New York Yankees and the Meaning of Life

Derek Gentile

MVP
BOOKS

First published in 2009 by MVP Books, an imprint of MBI Publishing Company and the Quayside Publishing Group, 400 First Avenue N, Suite 300, Minneapolis, MN 55401 USA

MVP Books are also available at discounts in bulk quantity for industrial or sales-promotional use. For details write to Special Sales Manager at Quayside Publishing, 400 First Avenue North, Suite 300, Minneapolis, MN 55401 USA.

Library of Congress Cataloging-in-Publication Data

Gentile, Derek.
  New York Yankees and the meaning of life / Derek Gentile.
    p. cm.
  ISBN 978-0-7603-3194-1 (plc)
  1. New York Yankees (Baseball team) I. Title.
  GV875.N4G455 2009
  796.357'64097471--dc22
                          2008039043

Editor: Josh Leventhal
Designer: Cindy Samargia Laun
Cover Design: Greg Nettles
Design Manager: Katie Sonmor

Printed in China

On the frontispiece: Casey Stengel, February 1949.

On the title page: Full moon over Yankee Stadium, Game Five, 1978 World Series.

Photo and Illustration Credits

We wish to acknowledge the following for providing the illustrations included in the book. Every effort has been made to locate the copyright holders for materials used, and we apologize for any oversights. Unless otherwise noted, all other images are from the publisher's collection.

AP/Wide World Photos: pp. 1, 50, 56, 66, 73, 75, 79, 86, 90, 94, 100, 117 (Preston Stroup), 118 (Bill Kostroun), 124, 128, 131, 145, 165 (Lorenzo Bevilaqua), 166 (Mike Derer), 169, 173, 181, 192, 201, 218, 221 (Ray Stubblebine), 224–225, 226, 228 (Ray Stubblebine), 230, 232 (Lennox McLendon), 234, 237 (Ray Stubblebine), 241 (Ray Stubblebine), 242, 245 (Ray Stubblebine), 252, 257 (Marty Lederhandler), 258, 260 (Marty Lerderhandler), 263, 264, 266, 269, 270, 273 (Harry Harris), 275 (Dave Pickoff), 278, 281 (Ray Stubblebine), 282, 285 (Harry Harris), 288 (Steve Pyle), 291, 295, 300 (Pat Sullivan), 303 (Cliff Schiappa), 304 (Ray Stubblebine), 307 (David Cantor), 308, 311 (Kathy Willens), 320 (Richard Harbus), 325 (John Dunn), 326 (Gene J. Puskar), 331 (David Zalubowski), 332 (Mark Lennihan), 335 (Roberto Borea), 339 (Eric Draper), 340 (Ron Frehm), 343 (Dave Hammond), 344 (Richard Drew), 349 (Ron Frehm), 351 (Mary Altaffer), 352 (Robert F. Bukaty), 355 (Julie Jacobson), 361 (Frances Roberts), 370 (Mark D. Phillips), 373 (Kathy Willens), 379 (Julie Jacobson), 380 (Julie Jacobson), 392 (Stephan Savoia), 395 (Kathy Willens), front cover inset (Bill Kostroun), back cover (Kathy Willens).

Getty Images: pp. 2 (Heinz Kluetmeier/*Sports Illustrated*), 54 (Louis Van Oeyen/Western Reserve Historical Society), 60 (Ralph Morse/Time Life Pictures), 133 (Arthur Rickerby/Diamond Images), 136 (Olen Collection/Diamond Images), 140 (Hulton Archive), 157 (Jeff Haynes/AFP), 189 (Hy Peskin/Time Life Pictures), 198 (Hy Peskin/Time Life Pictures), 207 (Olen Collection/Diamond Images), 210 (Olen Collection/Diamond Images), 213 (C&G Collections), 246 (Robert Riger), 255 (Focus on Sport), 297 (Tim Sloan/AFP), 299 (Olen Collection/Diamond Images), 317 (Jonathan Daniel), 346 (Vincent Laforet/Allsport), 358 (Chris Trotman), 363 (Olen Collection/Diamond Images), 369 (Kidwiler Collection/Diamond Images), 383 (Ezra Shaw).

George Brace Photo Collection: p. 385.

Library of Congress, Prints and Photographs Division: pp. 8–9, 387.

Library of Congress, Prints and Photographs Division, George Grantham Bain Collection: pp. 11, 12, 18, 34, 41, 134.

National Baseball Hall of Fame Library, Cooperstown, N.Y.: pp. 17, 25, 28, 31, 32, 38, 45, 46, 48, 63, 76, 99, 103, 106, 114, 122, 139, 150, 154, 158, 161, 170, 176, 179, 182, 186, 194, 197, 204, 208, 216, 222, 238, 248, 251, 276, 292, 315, 318, 323, 364, 391, 400.

Ponzini, Michael: pp. 328, 336.

Shutterstock.com: pp. 6, 22, 313, 377, 388, front cover background.

Transcendental Graphics/The Rucker Archive: pp. 14, 21, 26, 37, 42, 53, 65, 70, 80, 83, 85, 88, 92, 96, 109, 110, 112, 121, 153, 174, 184, 190, 214, 366.

Yablonsky, Bryan: p. 356.

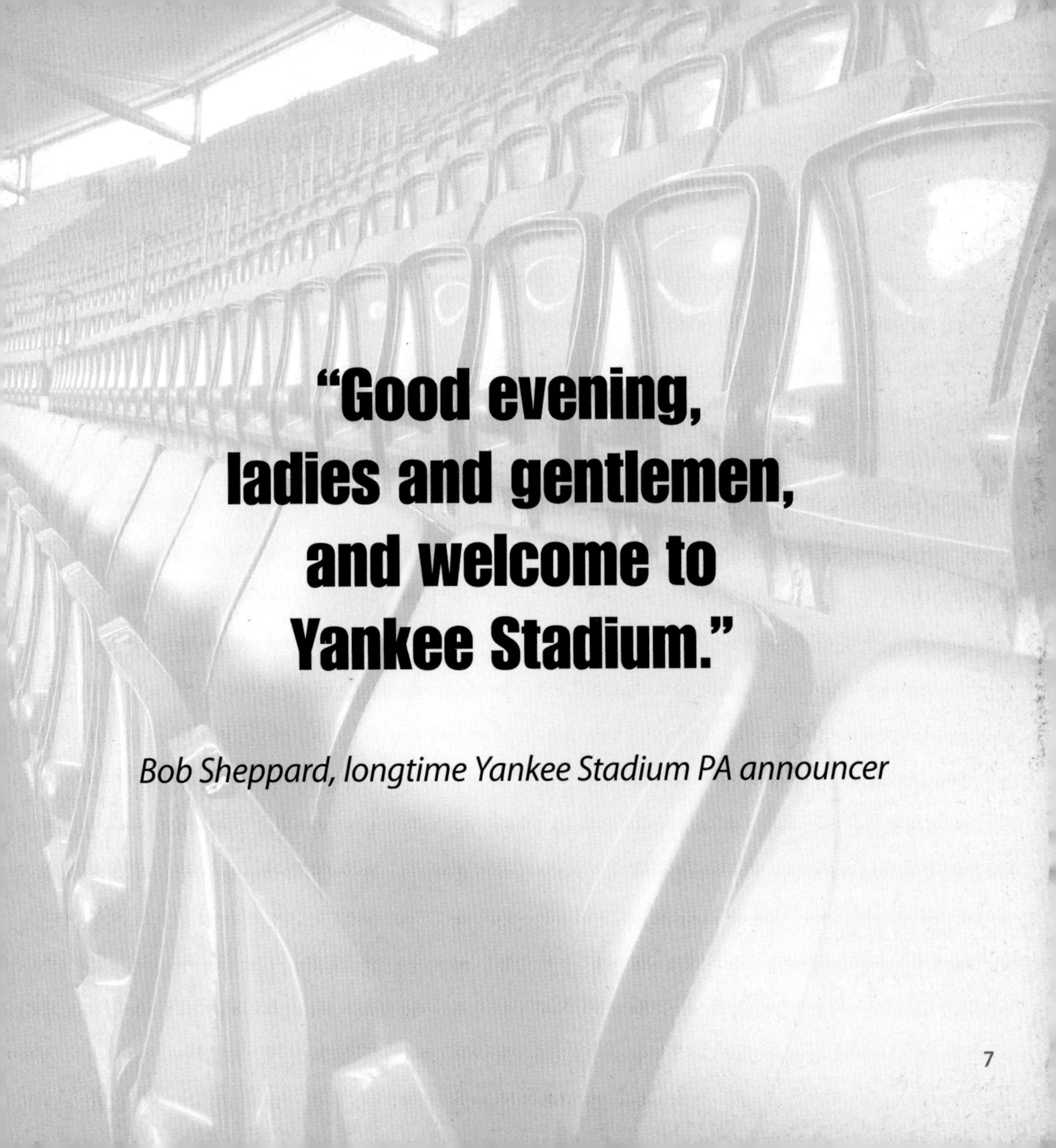

"Good evening,
ladies and gentlemen,
and welcome to
Yankee Stadium."

Bob Sheppard, longtime Yankee Stadium PA announcer

The Early Days: From Highlanders to Bronx Bombers

American League Park, New York.

Hilltop Park, home of the New York Highlanders, 1910

"I keep my eyes clear and I hit 'em where they ain't."

Wee Willie Keeler, on the secret to hitting

Willie Keeler, shown here batting at New York's Hilltop Park, was one of the great early stars of baseball and one of the best bunters of all time. He joined the Yankees—then known as the Highlanders—in 1903 and batted over .300 in each of his first four seasons with the team. He retired in 1910 with a lifetime average of .341.

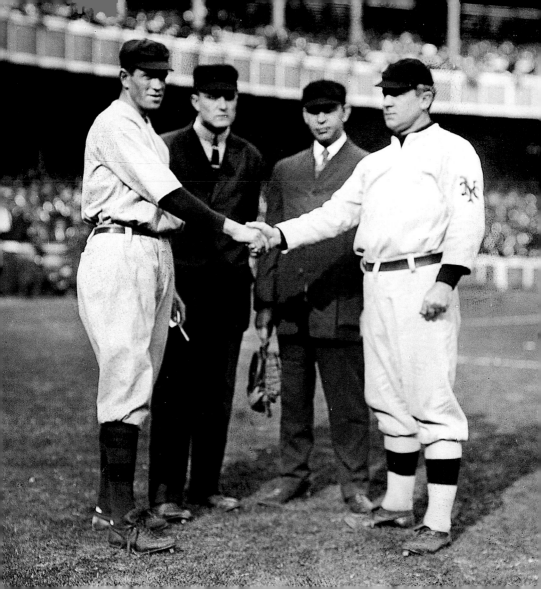

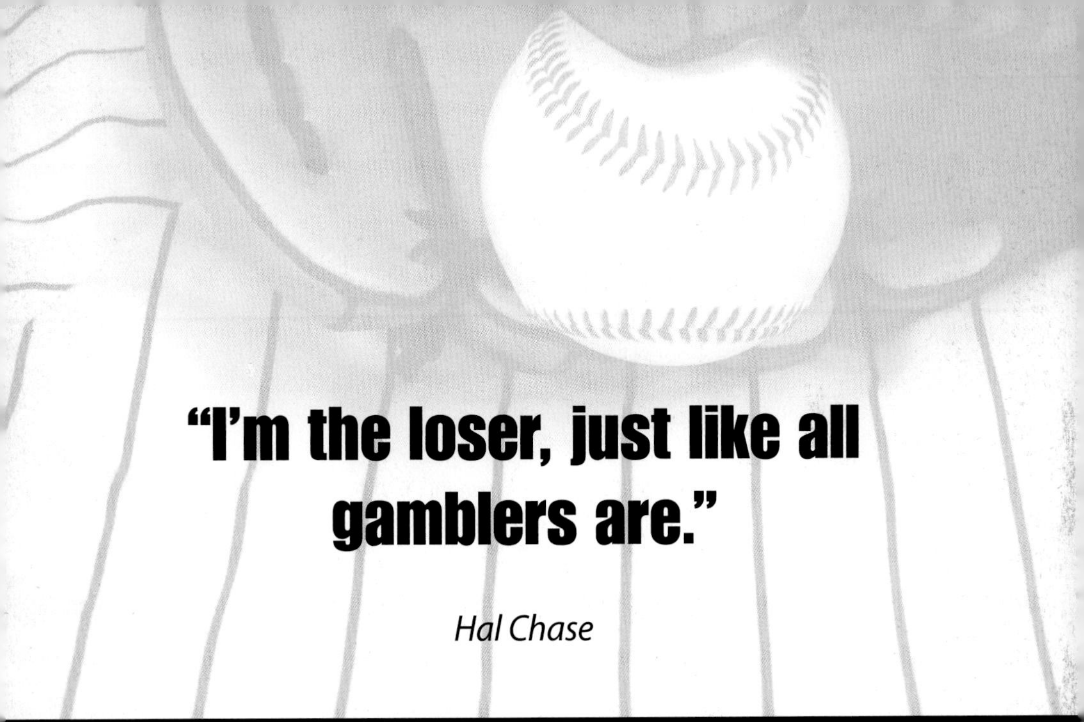

"I'm the loser, just like all gamblers are."

Hal Chase

"Prince" Hal Chase (left) starred for the New York Highlanders in the early 1900s and was also one of the game's most notorious gamblers. Betting was open and commonplace in baseball at the time. Gamblers frequented the hotels in which players stayed and the bars in which they drank, and for ballplayers, the temptation to gamble was tremendous. Chase didn't resist. He was ultimately banned from baseball for gambling and throwing games. He's shown here shaking hands with New York Giants manager John McGraw before a 1910 exhibition game.

"Coive him!
Coive the busher!"

Miller Huggins

Hall of Fame manager Miller Huggins—quoted here calling for a curveball in New York–ese—liked to harass and taunt opposing teams' rookies. Huggins became skipper of the New York Yankees in 1918 and went on to lead the team to six pennants and four championships, including the 1927 powerhouse that went 110–44. Huggins said the 1927 team was the greatest he ever saw, an assessment that is shared by many impartial observers.

"You ought to know that you're making a mistake."

Ed Barrow, to Red Sox owner Harry Frazee

In January 1920, against the wishes of Red Sox General Manager Ed Barrow, Harry Frazee sold Babe Ruth to the New York Yankees for $100,000. The error of Frazee's ways was made clear pretty quickly; Ruth blasted 54 homers in his first season with New York. Barrow came over to the Yankees in 1921 and served as general manager for more than two decades, helping to build one of sports' all-time dynasties. Ruth is pictured with Barrow (center) and Yankees owner Jacob Ruppert (right).

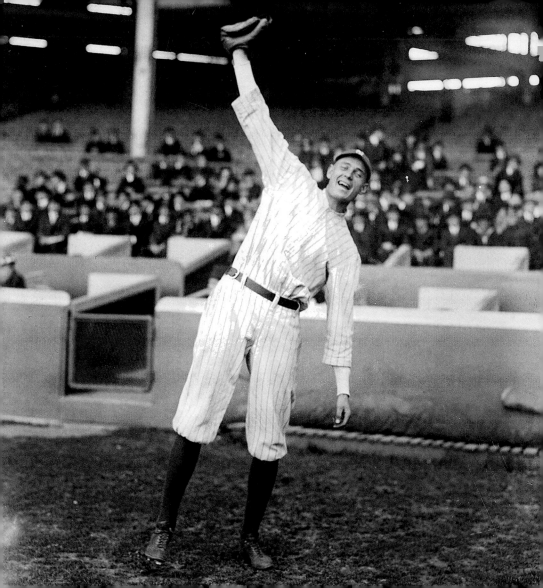

"I took the two most expensive aspirins in history."

Wally Pipp

Wally Pipp was an excellent first baseman who amassed nearly 2,000 hits and 1,000 RBI in his 15-year career. In 1925, Pipp was suffering from headaches after getting hit in the head by a ball and was replaced in the lineup by Lou Gehrig, who took position at first base—and didn't come out for another 2,130 games. Even if Pipp had not begged out of the lineup that day, with a legend-in-the-making waiting in the wings, Pipp's days in New York were numbered.

"It's great to be young and a Yankee!"

Waite Hoyt

That's not Waite Hoyt posing with Yankee legend Babe Ruth, but the future Hall of Fame pitcher was only 21 years old when he was traded to the Yankees from the Boston Red Sox in 1920. Hoyt spent the next nine seasons in New York, where he was a two-time 20-game winner and one of the best pitchers of his era. Hoyt was also a vaudeville actor and singer, and like his friend Ruth, he loved being in New York City.

"You got yourself into it. Now get yourself out of it!"

Tony Lazzeri, to Waite Hoyt

Second baseman Tony Lazzeri didn't have very encouraging words during a conference on the mound after Hoyt loaded the bases in a 1929 game. Hoyt recalled that, most of the time, mound conferences were pretty dull affairs in his day. Most managers didn't have much to say to pitchers, except "throw strikes." Trips to the mound by managers and coaches are a lot more common in today's game, and you'll often see nearly the entire team gathered on the mound for the discussion.

> **"It's always the same: Combs walks, Koenig singles, Ruth hits one out of the park, Gehrig doubles, Lazzeri triples. Then Dugan goes in the dirt on his can."**
>
> *Joe Dugan, explaining the Yankee batting order in 1927*

Joe Dugan, shown here relaxing on the Yankee bench, was the starting third baseman for all three Yankee championship teams of the 1920s. Dugan was known as "Jumpin' Joe"—not for his acrobatic defense, but because when he was with the Philadelphia Athletics, he would often "jump," or leave, the team for a few days. After joining the Yankees in 1922, he rarely, if ever, jumped the team.

> "They didn't get along. Gehrig thought Ruth was a big mouth and Ruth thought Gehrig was cheap. They were both right."

Tony Lazzeri

As Babe Ruth's teammate for nine seasons and Lou Gehrig's for twelve, Tony Lazzeri had plenty of insight into the relationship between the two Yankee legends. Ruth and Gehrig were each superstars in their own right, but their different backgrounds and lifestyles sometimes created tension between them. As the game's two biggest stars, they were often asked to pose for photos together, and they always put on a happy face in public.

The Sultan of Swat and the Iron Horse

Lou Gehrig and Babe Ruth

> ## "I swing big, with everything I've got. I hit big or I miss big. I like to live as big as I can."

Babe Ruth

The Babe wields a very big bat in this 1933 photo op with boxer Jack Dempsey. George Herman "Babe" Ruth revolutionized the game of baseball with his big-swinging, fun-loving ways. He was not only the best player of his era—and arguably of all time—he was also the sport's first pop-culture icon. More than 70 years after he played his last game, Ruth still ranks among the top ten all-time in home runs, RBI, runs, bases on balls, batting average, on-base percentage, and slugging percentage.

"If it wasn't for baseball, I'd be in the penitentiary or the cemetery."

Babe Ruth

By his own admission, Babe Ruth was a wild kid, roaming the streets of Baltimore while his parents worked in the family saloon. He attended a strict Catholic school and made his way onto the baseball team. When he was just 19 years old, he was signed by the Boston Red Sox to a professional baseball contract. By the early 1920s, the only fences around Ruth were between him and his legions of fans.

"If he plays every day, that bum will hit into 100 double plays a season."

John McGraw, on Babe Ruth, in 1917

Babe Ruth was a dominating hurler for the Boston Red Sox before the team started using him as an outfielder. New York Giants manager John McGraw, for one, was skeptical about the Babe's conversion to everyday player. After he became a Yankee, Ruth regularly faced the Giants in exhibitions, and every time Ruth hit a home run in one of those games, he'd look over at McGraw and shout, "Another double-play ball, eh, Johnny?" The two are pictured together in the early 1920s.

"I hope he lives to hit 100 home runs in a season. I wish him all the luck in the world. He has everyone else, including myself, hopelessly outclassed."

Frank "Home Run" Baker, on Babe Ruth

Frank Baker earned his nickname for belting 2 home runs during the 1911 World Series as a member of the Philadelphia Athletics, but he never hit more than 12 in a season and had only 96 in his entire career. In 1920, his first season with the Yankees, Ruth hit 54 home runs—more than any other *team* in the American League. Baker (right) stands with his legendary teammate before a 1921 contest.

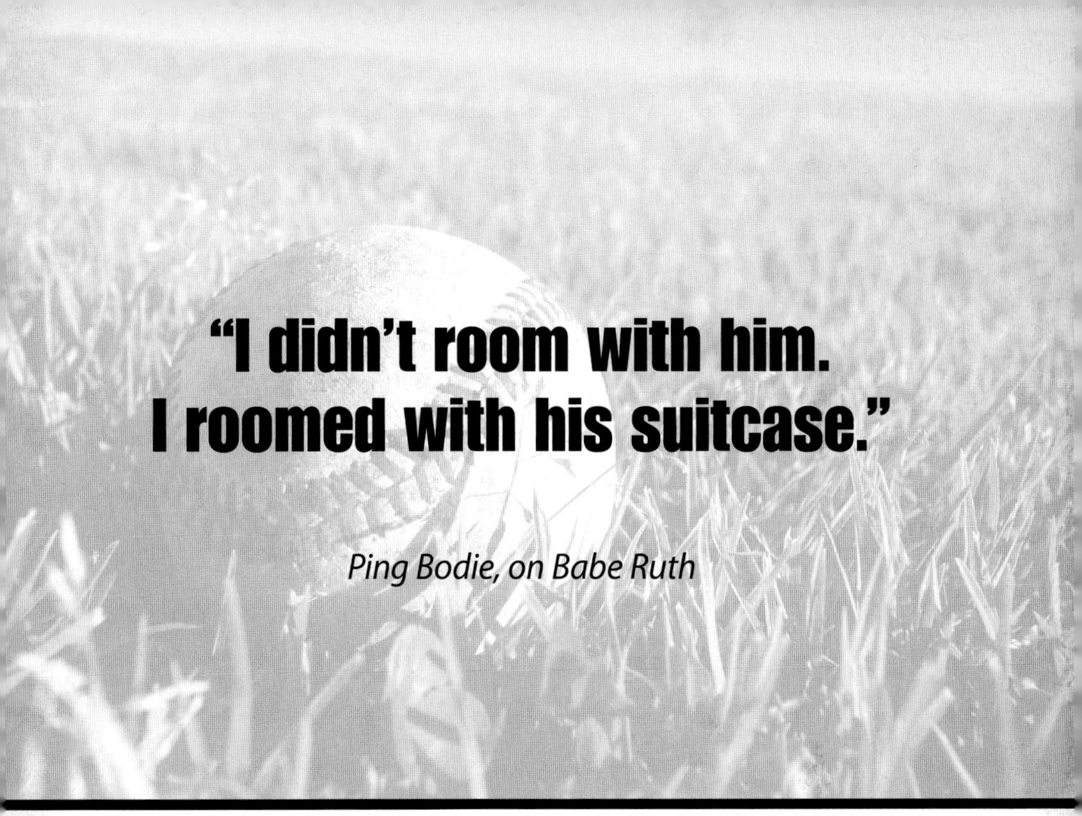

"I didn't room with him. I roomed with his suitcase."

Ping Bodie, on Babe Ruth

The Babe—seen here surrounded by a bunch of, well, babes—was well known as a ladies' man. Ping Bodie was Ruth's roommate when Ruth came to New York in 1920. This famous quote was from a small sidebar story by a beat reporter that season. The reporter had to ask Bodie several times what it was like to room with his new teammate because Bodie was reluctant to admit that Ruth, already the darling of New York, was something of a wild man.

"I had a better year than he did."

Babe Ruth

Ruth's defense of why he was earning more money than President Herbert Hoover illustrates his lack of self-consciousness about his salary or his abilities. As far as he was concerned, whatever he could wrangle out of the Yankees was fair, given that he was the team's biggest star, and the team was the best in baseball. Herbert Hoover, meanwhile, led the nation into the Great Depression. Ruth also had many better years than President Warren Harding, whom he greets before a 1923 game at Yankee Stadium.

"Whenever I hit a home run, I make certain I touch all the bases."

Babe Ruth

That was Ruth's response to the question of whether he had any superstitions, and the "Sultan of Swat" made sure to touch all the bases 714 times in his career—a record that stood for nearly four decades, when Hank Aaron broke it. Not just a one-dimensional slugger, Ruth also hit plenty of singles, doubles, and triples in his career and was known to steal a few bases in his younger days.

"Every big leaguer and his wife should teach their children to pray, 'God bless Mommy, God bless Daddy, and God bless Babe Ruth.'"

Waite Hoyt

Waite Hoyt (left) was Babe Ruth's teammate for nearly a decade, during which time he won 157 games and played on three World Series champions. Thanks in large part to Ruth and the rest of Murderer's Row, Hoyt went 6–3 in the Fall Classic, including two victories in the 1928 series—a series in which Ruth batted .625 with three home runs. Hoyt later wrote a book called *Babe Ruth as I Knew Him* that is packed with anecdotes about his famous teammate.

"He hits a ball harder and farther than any man I ever saw."

Bill Dickey, on Babe Ruth

Bill Dickey, who was Ruth's teammate between 1928 and 1934, was one of several Yankees who swore that when Ruth hit the ball, it actually sounded different, making a deeper, harder cracking sound. Dickey could hit the ball pretty well himself. A career .313 hitter, he belted at least 20 homers, drove in more than 100 runs, and batted over .300 in every season from 1936 to 1939—all championship years for New York.

"Sixty! Count 'em, 60! Let's see someone top that!"

Babe Ruth, after hitting his 60th home run in 1927

It would be 34 years before someone did top Ruth's record of 60 homers in a season. He hit number 60 on September 30, 1927, against Washington pitcher Tom Zachary at Yankee Stadium. Ruth's homer that day was curving foul down the right field line, and after it went into the stands, Zachary screamed that it was foul. Zachary, who joined Ruth's Yankees in 1928, was present for the Babe Ruth Day celebration at the Stadium in 1947. As Zachary went to shake the Bambino's hand, Ruth said, "You crooked-armed son of a bitch, are you still telling people that ball was foul?"

"I'd play for half my salary if I could hit in this dump all the time."

Babe Ruth, on Chicago's Wrigley Field

Ruth and the Yankees got a chance to hit in Wrigley Field during the 1932 World Series. The third game of that series was the occasion of Ruth's legendary "called shot." He most likely didn't actually call his shot, but after Chicago pitcher Charlie Root got two strikes on him, he pointed to Root with one finger and said, "It only takes one to hit it!" And then he hit it. In the photo, he's approaching the plate after hitting the first of his two home runs that day.

"Don't be afraid to take advice. There's always something new to learn."

Babe Ruth

Ruth offers advice to a couple of youngsters on the cover of *Babe Ruth's Baseball Advice* magazine. Here, he provides instruction on bunting, not exactly his specialty. Ruth enjoyed sharing his knowledge and desperately wanted to become a baseball manager. In 1935, he joined the last-place Boston Braves, expecting to be offered the managerial job for the following year, but he never got the call.

Babe Ruth's
BASEBALL ADVICE

"To hell with newspapermen. You can buy them with a steak."

George Weiss

Well, maybe that was true, but Babe Ruth still enjoyed catching up on the day's sports news in the local papers. Ruth always got along with sportswriters, but George Weiss, who was a Yankee front-office executive for nearly 30 years, believed that sportswriters served no real purpose. Had they merely reported the scores of the ballgames, Weiss might have been a little more sanguine. But to Weiss, sportswriters were spreaders of bad rumors and misinformation.

"He had such a beautiful swing. He even looked good striking out."

Mark Koenig, on Babe Ruth

As the Yankee shortstop from 1925 to 1929, Mark Koenig saw a lot of beautiful swings by the mighty Babe, and not all of them resulted in home runs. While Ruth collected 2,873 hits in his career, he also struck out 1,330 times—which stood as the all-time record until Mickey Mantle broke it in 1963. Here Ruth takes a big cut during batting practice in 1929.

> # "All ballplayers should quit when it starts to feel as if the baselines run uphill."

Babe Ruth

A veteran Ruth checks out the action from the Yankee dugout late in his career. After 15 seasons with the Yankees, the 40-year-old Ruth signed with the Boston Braves for the 1935 season. He appeared in only 28 games before hanging up the spikes for good. In one of his final appearances as a player, the Bambino belted three homers in a game against the Pittsburgh Pirates, including one that cleared the Forbes Field roof.

"Baseball was, is, and always will be to me the greatest game in the world."

Babe Ruth, on Babe Ruth Day

On April 27, 1947, an ailing Babe Ruth, suffering from cancer, was honored by his former team at Yankee Stadium with a capacity crowd of more than sixty thousand in attendance. He made his final appearance at the stadium a year later, shortly before he died, on August 16, 1948, at the age of 53. An all-time legend, Ruth's impact on the game of baseball cannot be overstated.

> ## "The greatest name in American sports history is Babe Ruth, a hitter."

Ted Williams

Two all-time greats: The Bambino and the Splendid Splinter. Boston Red Sox legend Ted Williams, the last major leaguer to bat over .400 in a season, knew a thing or two about hitting himself, and he is often included, along with Ruth, in any discussion of the game's all-time best. But while Ruth won eight World Series titles in his 21 seasons with the Yankees and Red Sox, Williams never knew the team success that the Babe enjoyed.

> "Honestly, at one time I thought Babe Ruth was a cartoon character. I mean, I wasn't born until 1961, and I grew up in Indiana."

Don Mattingly

Ruth's image appeared in many forms, even to sell undergarments, and he was a larger-than-life figure to millions of Americans. Don Mattingly eventually figured things out by the time he joined the Yankees in 1982. While his numbers were not quite Ruthian, Mattingly won a batting crown in 1984 and followed that with an MVP season in 1985. He played 14 seasons in New York (1982–1995) but never once made it to the World Series.

"It's a pretty big shadow, but it gives me lots of room to spread myself."

Lou Gehrig, on playing with Babe Ruth

Playing alongside Ruth often left Lou Gehrig toiling in relative obscurity, but it was a two-way street, as he was somewhat protected from criticism because all eyes were on Ruth. Of course, there wasn't much to criticize with Gehrig, even after his larger-than-life teammate left the Yankees in 1935. When Gehrig retired in 1939, he ranked second in career home runs (trailing only Ruth), third in runs batted in, and second (to Ruth) in slugging percentage.

"There was absolutely no reason to dislike him, and nobody did."

Sportswriter Fred Lieb, on Lou Gehrig

The "Iron Horse" wasn't completely without sin and was known to enjoy a cold brew and a smoke now and again, even in the locker room after a game—but Lou Gehrig was widely respected by teammates and opponents alike. His streak of 2,130 consecutive games played was a testament to his dedication to the game, and it stood as a record for more than a half century, until Cal Ripken Jr. broke it in 1995.

"Lou Gehrig never learned that a ballplayer couldn't be good every day."

Hank Gowdy

Hank Gowdy, a 17-year major league veteran, was one of many ballplayers who marveled at Gehrig's consistency. Day in and day out, year in and year out, the guy was an offensive machine, as is evident in the numbers: 13 consecutive seasons with 100 runs and 100 RBI, 12 consecutive seasons batting over .300, 12 consecutive seasons with at least 25 home runs, and 9 straight seasons with at least 30 homers.

"In the beginning, I used to make one terrible play a game. Then I got so I'd make one a week, and finally I'd pull a bad one about once a month. Now, I'm trying to keep it down to one a season."

Lou Gehrig

Gehrig may have been a bit clumsy playing first base initially, but he got better as his career progressed. Although he was never a defensive standout and is best known for his hitting prowess, he was more graceful with the glove than many of his contemporaries.

"The ballplayer who loses his head, who can't keep his cool, is worse than no ballplayer at all."

Lou Gehrig

Gehrig kept his cool in this argument with umpire George Moriarity during a 1937 game in Philadelphia, and he convinced Moriarity to reverse the ruling. Gehrig used his level head to become a dominating hitter and on-field leader. He was in the running for the Most Valuable Player Award in practically every season he played.

"Joe, I'm not helping the team any. I know I look terrible out there."

Lou Gehrig, to manager Joe McCarthy

On May 2, 1939, Gehrig asked out of the lineup after 2,130 consecutive games played. A few days afterward, Gehrig and Joe McCarthy smiled for the cameras, but both men were in agony. Gehrig, at the time, did not know what was wrong. Rumors were running rampant that he had an exotic illness, such as malaria or some kind of contagious infection. McCarthy knew that he was in danger of losing not only a star player, but also a good friend.

"Maybe the rest will help. Who knows?"

Lou Gehrig

Speaking to reporters after missing his first game since 1925, Gehrig had no idea that he had played his last game, and neither did anyone else. Still, the Hall of Fame first baseman had a front-row seat as the 1939 Yankees went on to be one of the best teams of all time, despite his absence from the lineup.

BETTING PROHIBITED

CLEVE	0 0 0
DETRT	0 0 0
CHIGO	
ST.LOU	
BOST	4 0 6 0 0
PHILA	0 0 3 1 3
WASH	
YANKS	

AT BAT
0

UMPIRES · PLAT

"Fans, for the past two weeks you have been reading about a bad break I got. Yet today, I consider myself the luckiest man on the face of the earth."

Lou Gehrig

On July 4, 1939, the "Iron Horse" gave a memorable farewell speech to a packed crowd at Yankee Stadium on Lou Gehrig Appreciation Day. Even the most casual baseball fan knows this speech, one of the most moving moments in baseball history and memorably depicted in the classic baseball movie, *Pride of the Yankees*. One of the saddest things about Gehrig's disease was how it cut down a vigorous man in the prime of his life.

"There is no room in baseball for discrimination. It is our national pastime and a game for all."

Lou Gehrig

Gehrig was an early voice to speak out against segregation in baseball, and he often played exhibition games with African-American ballplayers. He was always supportive of the caliber of play in the Negro Leagues, but it was not until 1947, nearly six years after Gehrig's death, that an African American would play in the majors. Organized leagues for black players had been around since the 1880s, and here the Baltimore Blues pose for a team portrait as the "Colored Champions of Maryland."

DUVAL, P.   PINDER, L. F.   FEGGANS, P.   RODGERS, Pres. R.F.
SAVOY, C. F.   REYNOLDS, 2nd B.   JORDON, Mngr.   RANKINS, 1st B.   COLDER, 3rd B.
WILLIS, Sub.   FARRELL, Capt. & C.   HILL, S. S.

The Baltimore Blues Base-ball Club.
Colored Champions of Maryland.

Joltin' Joe and the Next Yankee Dynasty

Manager Joe McCarthy, Lou Gehrig, Red Ruffing, Lefty Gomez, Joe DiMaggio, Bill Dickey, and Red Rolfe in 1938

"Let me do the worrying."

Joe McCarthy, to sportswriters

Manager Joe McCarthy; owner Colonel Jacob Ruppert; and players Joe DiMaggio, Lou Gehrig, and Tony Lazzeri appear a little worried as they face the media in October 1937. But the Yankees had just won their second consecutive World Series, defeating the New York Giants four games to two. Still, New York was a tough place to play, even in the 1930s, and the Yankees were always under the media spotlight.

"A catcher must want to catch. He must make up his mind that it isn't the terrible job it is painted and that he isn't going to say every day, 'Why oh why, with so many other positions in baseball did I take up this one?'"

Bill Dickey

Bill Dickey took up the catcher's position for 1,708 regular-season games in his career, plus 38 in the World Series. In 81 other regular season games, he appeared as a pinch-hitter. He never played another position in 1,827 total games with the Yankees. Such resilience earned him 11 all-star selections and a plaque in Cooperstown. He also managed the team for much of the 1946 season while serving as a reserve catcher.

"I loved to make a great defensive play. I'd rather do that than hit a home run."

Bill Dickey

Dickey was among the best at his position and led the American League in fielding percentage four times. He could also hit home runs, which he did 202 times in his career, and his 29 homers in 1937 stood as the single-season record for American League catchers until it was broken by his successor, Yogi Berra, in 1952.

"The secret of my success was clean living and a fast outfield."

Lefty Gomez

Vernon "Lefty" Gomez had no illusions about his abilities. He had a good array of pitches, but as he conceded, the powerful Yankee lineup would occasionally bail him out with a four- or five-run inning. Still, Gomez led the league in ERA twice (1933 and 1937) while also leading in strikeouts and wins in both seasons. He was the American League starter in five All-Star Games and had a perfect 5–0 record in World Series play.

"You keep the salary, I'll take the cut."

Lefty Gomez

Lefty Gomez had this snappy response to owner Jacob Ruppert's news that Gomez's $20,000 salary was being cut by $12,500 to $7,500. He eventually agreed to re-sign with the team, and he even bares a smile as he signs the contract at spring training in March 1934, alongside manager Joe McCarthy.

"I am throwing twice as hard as I ever did. It's just not getting there as fast."

Lefty Gomez

After 13 years in a Yankee uniform, the 33-year-old Gomez was let go by New York after the 1942 season. (He resurfaced to start one game for the Washington Senators in 1943 but lasted less than five innings.) Today, Gomez ranks third on the all-time Yankee franchise list in games won (189) and is fourth in innings pitched.

"I talked to the ball a lot of times in my career. I'd yell, 'Go foul! Go foul!'"

Lefty Gomez

In addition to being a Hall of Fame pitcher, the colorful Lefty Gomez was also a legendary quipster. After his playing days, he was often invited for speaking engagements to share his baseball stories and humor. The California native also married the musical-comedy actress June O'Dea.

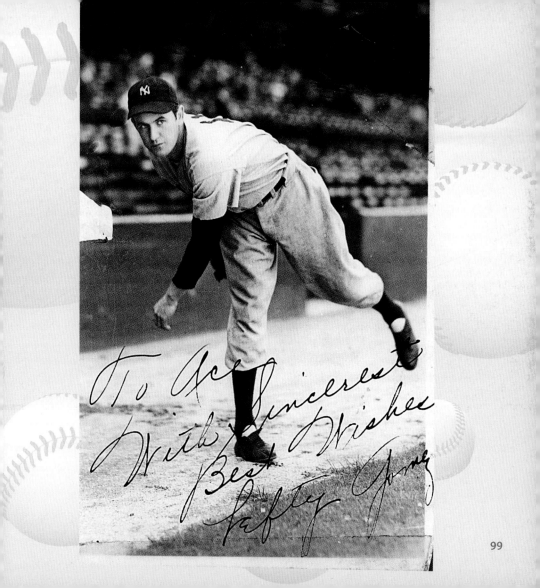

To Ace
With Sincerest
Best Wishes
Lefty Grove

"You've bought yourself a cripple."

Bill Terry, after the Yankees signed Joe DiMaggio

Bill Terry, a Hall of Fame first baseman, had doubts about Yankee prospect Joe DiMaggio. The young outfielder had injured his knee while playing for the San Francisco Seals of the Pacific Coast League, and there was concern that he might be damaged goods. Manager Joe McCarthy didn't seem too concerned at spring training in March 1936. The rookie DiMaggio went on to play in 138 games and collect 206 hits, 29 homers, 125 runs batted in, and a .323 average. He only got better from there.

"There is always some kid who may be seeing me for the first or last time. I owe him my best."

Joe DiMaggio

Joe DiMaggio always gave his best—at the plate, in the field, and on the base paths—and he was always willing to sign autographs for his fans. The three-time American League Most Valuable Player was selected to the All-Star Game every season he was in the league. A lifetime .325 hitter, DiMaggio could hit for power and was one of the toughest guys to strike out.

"I can remember a reporter asking me for a quote. I didn't know what a quote was. I thought it was some kind of soft drink."

Joe DiMaggio, on his rookie year

Joe DiMaggio was soft-spoken and a bit shy as a young major leaguer. Some reporters came to calling him "Dead-Pan Joe" for his superficial, monosyllabic responses to questions. As he matured and became a celebrity under the bright lights of New York City, DiMaggio learned how to handle the media and usually had a good rapport with the writers.

> ## "The phrase, 'Off with the crack of the bat,' while romantic, is really meaningless since the outfielder should be in motion long before he hears the sound of the ball meeting the bat."
>
> *Joe DiMaggio, on outfield play*

Joe DiMaggio, seen here making a nice catch, always appeared graceful in the outfield. For 13 seasons, "Joltin' Joe" roamed the vast expanses of the Yankee Stadium center field, always anticipating where the ball was headed and rarely making a mental error. In 1947, he committed only one error in 139 games.

"I can't say I'm glad it's over. Of course, I wanted it to go on as long as it could."

Joe DiMaggio, on his 56-game hitting streak

Joe DiMaggio's 56-game hitting streak in 1941 still stands as the longest streak in major league history. Although Boston's Ted Williams hit .406 that season, DiMaggio was named the league's Most Valuable Player for 1941. To Williams' credit, he said in an interview years later that DiMaggio deserved the award. The year also saw DiMaggio and the Yankees win their fifth World Series in six years.

"It's got to be better than rooming with Joe Page."

Joe DiMaggio, on his marriage to Marilyn Monroe

Already a cultural icon beyond the baseball diamond, DiMaggio's celebrity status went up a notch when he married Marilyn Monroe in 1954. The marriage was brief, lasting only nine months, but it is said that DiMaggio always carried a torch for his ex-wife. (His relationship with Joe Page lasted five years, as members of the Yankees from 1946 to 1950.)

"There was never a day when I was as good as Joe DiMaggio at his best. Joe was the best, the very best I ever saw."

Stan Musial

"Joe DiMaggio was the greatest all-around player I ever saw."

Ted Williams

Stan Musial, Ted Williams, and Joe DiMaggio were three of the greatest players in baseball history, and they dominated during the 1940s. At the 1938 All-Star Game, DiMaggio posed with some other baseball legends (left to right): Lou Gehrig, Joe Cronin, Bill Dickey, DiMaggio, Charlie Gehringer, Jimmy Foxx, and Hank Greenberg.

"Baseball isn't statistics. It's Joe DiMaggio rounding second base."

Jimmy Breslin

DiMaggio's grace, professionalism, work ethic, and all-around talent exemplified baseball at its best. In 1969, at baseball's centennial celebration, he was proclaimed "baseball's greatest living player." Had he not lost three full seasons to World War II and had several seasons cut short by injuries, DiMaggio's statistics would be even more impressive than they already are.

"He did everything so naturally that half the time he gave the impression he wasn't trying. He made the rest of them look like plumbers."

Casey Stengel, on DiMaggio

DiMaggio was a natural, but he still worked hard to be the best he could be. And like a good plumber, he made sure to take care of his equipment. In 1949, Casey Stengel's first year as Yankee manager, DiMaggio played in only 76 games because of injuries, but he still helped lead the team to a World Series. The Hall of Fame manager occasionally butted heads with his star player, but the pair teamed up to win three straight championships (1949–1951).

> **"You always get a special kick on Opening Day, no matter how many you go through. You look forward to it like a birthday party when you're a kid. You think something wonderful is going to happen."**

Joe DiMaggio

"Joltin' Joe" enjoyed 13 Opening Days as a player, and he often returned to Yankee Stadium for celebrations after he retired. One of the most popular players ever to wear a Yankee uniform, he was on hand to deliver the ceremonial first pitch on Opening Day in 1994. DiMaggio's number 5 was retired after his final season as a player, and he was honored at Yankee Stadium's Monument Park with a plaque in 1969, which was replaced by a full monument after his death in 1999.

The Old Perfessor: Casey Stengel

"The Yankees don't pay me to win every day. Just two out of three."

Casey Stengel

Casey's Yankees didn't win every day, but to the rest of the American League, it sure seemed like it. In 12 seasons as the Yankee skipper (1949–1960), Stengel had a combined winning percentage of .623, and the team won 10 pennants and 7 World Series. Here, Stengel celebrates with his players after clinching his first championship in New York.

"The secret of managing is to keep the guys who hate you away from the guys who are undecided."

Casey Stengel

Stengel prepares all his players—those who hate him and the undecided—at spring training in St. Petersburg, Florida, before the 1950 season. The Yankees were coming off a championship in 1949, the first season with Stengel at the helm. They would win another World Series in 1950. And 1951. And 1952. And 1953. The five consecutive championships have never been equaled by any other team, Yankee or otherwise. Perhaps "The Old Perfessor" had indeed found the secret of managing.

"Most ballgames are lost, not won."

Casey Stengel

Another classic Stengelism that reveals how well Casey understood the game of baseball. Although he was known as a jokester even back in his playing days, Stengel's mastery of the game of baseball was unparalleled. He enjoyed sharing his words of wisdom with his players, and the results were mostly successful. He maintained a good relationship with his charges as well as with the media, who were always happy to print a Stengel quote or photograph.

WORDS OF WISDOM

"Son, we'd like to keep you around this season, but we're trying to win a pennant."

*Casey Stengel, to a Yankee prospect
who wasn't quite working out*

Casey Stengel was always on the lookout for top talent, and he could be cruel to young prospects if they didn't pan out quickly. There was a lot of pressure to succeed in New York, and Stengel was never one to accept mediocrity. Here he checks out the list of Yankee players and prospects before the start of his first spring training with the team in 1949.

"Kid, you're too small. You ought to go out and shine shoes."

Casey Stengel, to Phil Rizzuto

Stengel didn't exactly offer words of encouragement to shortstop Phil Rizzuto, but "Scooter" overcame the doubts and spent more than a dozen seasons with the Yankees en route to a Hall of Fame career. Here, the two enjoy a lighter moment after Rizzuto signed a new contract in November 1950 following his MVP season.

"Look at him. He doesn't drink, he doesn't smoke, he doesn't chew, he doesn't stay out late, and he still can't hit .250."

Casey Stengel, on Bobby Richardson

Clean-living Bobby Richardson, seen here fielding a pop-up during the 1960 World Series, was in the Yankee lineup mainly for his defense, and he was able to stay in the lineup for a decade. His career average was, in fact, .266, and only twice in his career did he hit below .250. The five-time Gold Glove winner also holds the record for most RBI in a single World Series, with 12 in 1960.

"What do you think, I was born old?"

Casey Stengel, to Mickey Mantle

Mickey Mantle might have been surprised to learn that his manager had played at Ebbets Field, but the young Stengel—shown here hamming it up as a member of the Brooklyn Dodgers in 1916—was a pretty fair ballplayer in his day. He helped the Giants win the 1922 world championship, and in 1923, Stengel hit the first World Series home run in Yankee Stadium.

"Managing is getting paid for home runs someone else hits."

Casey Stengel

This crew hit plenty of home runs for their manager (left to right): Roger Maris, Yogi Berra, Mickey Mantle, and Bill "Moose" Skowron. However, Stengel did not get paid for Maris' record-breaking home run campaign in 1961, having been fired after the previous year's World Series. Stengel's detractors often said that anyone could have won with the talent he had, but his five consecutive World Series wins are unmatched in baseball history.

"You have to have a catcher, or you'll have all passed balls."

Casey Stengel, on catching

Stengel had one of the game's great all-time catchers—and Stengel's peer for quotability—in Lawrence Peter "Yogi" Berra. This manager-catcher pair won seven championships together. Stengel holds the all-time record for World Series appearances by a manager (10 years), while Berra holds the record for players (14).

"Nobody ever had too many of them."

Casey Stengel, on pitchers

The Yankee manager is pictured with three of his star pitchers of the early 1950s: (left to right) Ed Lopat, Stengel, Vic Raschi, and Allie Reynolds. Lopat pitched for New York from 1948 to 1955, Raschi from 1946 to 1953, and Reynolds from 1947 to 1954. In 1951, Lopat and Raschi each won 21 games while Reynolds chipped in with 17 during that championship season.

"They told me my services are no longer desired because they wanted to put in a youth program. I'll never make the mistake of being 70 again."

Casey Stengel

After 12 straight winning seasons and 10 first-place finishes, Stengel was relieved of his duties after the 1960 World Series, when the Yankees lost to the Pittsburgh Pirates. He returned to manage in New York two years later, but with the lowly expansion New York Mets.

Unintentional Comedian: Yogi Berra

"They say he's funny. Well, he has a lovely wife and family, a beautiful home, money in the bank, and he plays golf with millionaires. What's funny about that?"

Casey Stengel, on Yogi Berra

Yogi Berra seems to be enjoying the good life at Yogi Berra Day in 1959. Manager Casey Stengel defended Berra in response to the media's portrayal of the Yankee catcher as a goofy boob. Stengel, and eventually most of the baseball world, recognized Berra as an elite talent. His three MVP Awards, 15 consecutive all-star selections, and Hall of Fame plaque are no laughing matter.

"Baseball is 90 percent mental. The other half is physical."

Yogi Berra

Berra used both his physical skills and his mental capacities over more than 40 years as a player, coach, and manager in the major leagues—most of them with the Yankees and most of them as a winner. He appeared in 14 World Series as a player and 2 as a manager. Playing behind the plate in nearly 1,700 regular-season games, Berra commanded all-star pitching staffs on many world champion teams.

NEWS WEEKLY · AUG. 4, 1952

10¢

Quick

YOGI BERRA

Baseball's
Roughest
Plays

NATURAL CHILDBIRTH — Success or Failure?

"He'd fall in a sewer and come up with a gold watch."

Casey Stengel, on Yogi Berra

Berra didn't get a gold watch on this trip to Cooperstown in 1972, but he was honored with a plaque in the Baseball Hall of Fame. (He's posing with Commissioner Bowie Kuhn.) Berra was one of those guys who always seemed to make the right play at the right time. As a key piece on a formidable baseball dynasty for nearly two decades, Yogi came up with plenty of jewelry: ten World Series rings and three MVP Awards.

"So I'm ugly. I never saw anyone hit with his face."

Yogi Berra

While it's true that he didn't exactly have matinee-idol good looks, Berra did have one of the most recognizable faces in baseball. And it didn't seem to matter much on the diamond—especially considering he spent much of his career wearing a mask.

"All pitchers are liars or crybabies."

Yogi Berra

Yogi surely wasn't talking about *Yankee* pitchers, and certainly not Whitey Ford, one of his favorite pitchers. Berra was behind the plate for most of Ford's wins during the first decade of the lefty pitcher's Hall of Fame career. Although, it's true that Whitey lied about his spitball—Ford was widely known as a purveyor of the illicit pitch.

"I always thought that record would stand until it was broken."

Yogi Berra, to Johnny Bench

Berra was one of the best hitting catchers in history, and he retired with more lifetime home runs as a catcher (306) than anyone else at the position. The record stood until it was broken by Cincinnati's star catcher, Johnny Bench, in 1980. Berra and Bench were selected as the two catchers for the Major League Baseball All-Century Team in 1999.

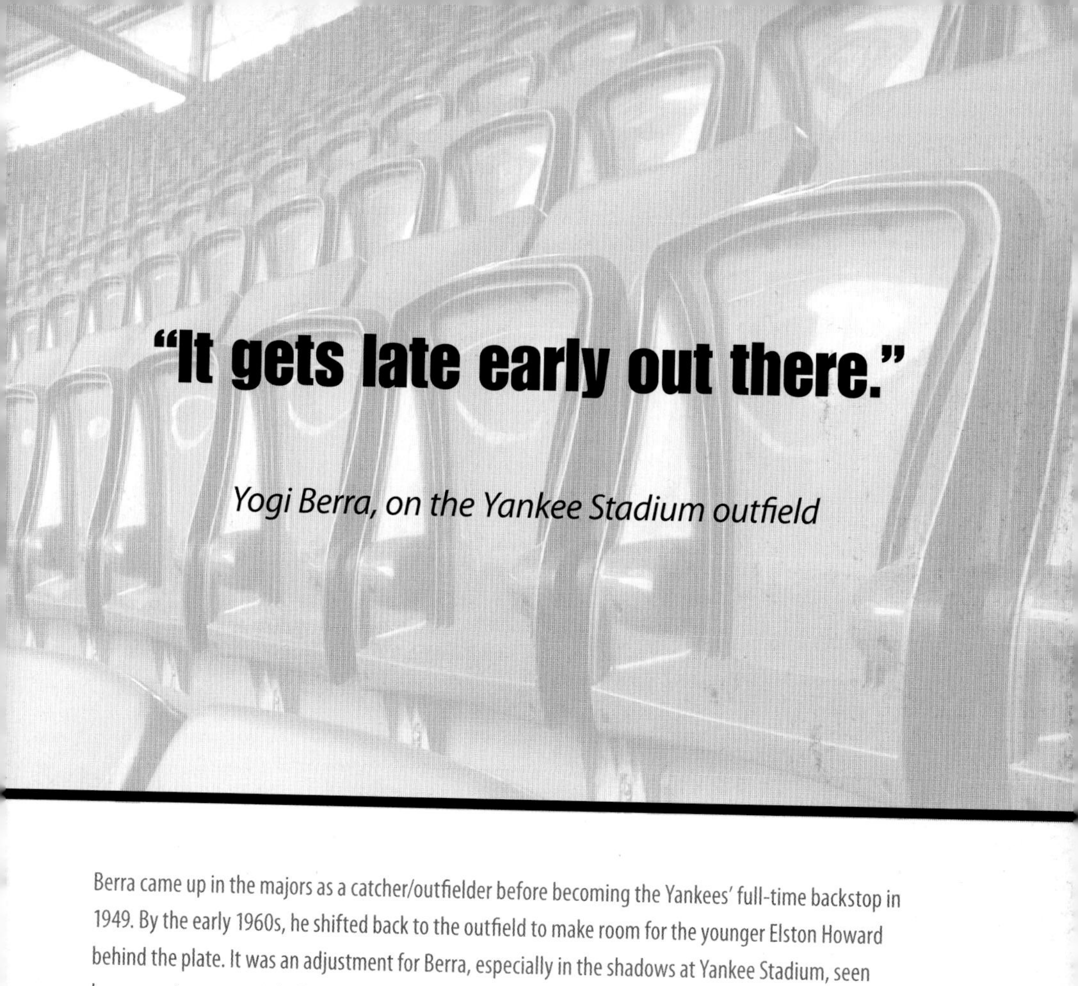

"It gets late early out there."

Yogi Berra, on the Yankee Stadium outfield

Berra came up in the majors as a catcher/outfielder before becoming the Yankees' full-time backstop in 1949. By the early 1960s, he shifted back to the outfield to make room for the younger Elston Howard behind the plate. It was an adjustment for Berra, especially in the shadows at Yankee Stadium, seen here creeping across right field.

"When you see a fork in the road, take it."

Yogi Berra

Berra always claimed that this line, which was part of the directions to his home, was perfectly clear and made sense when you followed it. Still, there's a definite Yogi element to the quote, and it almost sounds like meaningful words of wisdom. Here, Berra takes a fork in the road on a scooter.

"If people don't come out to the ballpark, who's going to stop them?"

Yogi Berra

Nobody was stopping fans from not coming out to Yankee Stadium in the late 1960s and early 1970s. After 40 consecutive seasons with the highest or second-highest attendance in the American League, the Yankees dropped to fourth in 1966 and didn't regain their place as attendance leaders until they started winning pennants a decade later. In 1972, season attendance dropped below one million for the first (and only) time since the end of World War II.

"It's déjà vu all over again."

Yogi Berra

Berra is posing with actor Joe Grifasi, who played him in the 2007 miniseries *The Bronx Is Burning*. This is one of the most famous Yogi Berra–isms, and Berra freely admitted that French was not his second language.

"I really didn't say most of the things I said."

Yogi Berra

Even in his attempt to explain that he never actually said many of the things he is credited with saying, Berra created a whole new Yogi-ism. In 1996, he received an honorary Doctor of Letters degree from Montclair State University in New Jersey. Dr. Berra's parting remarks to the student body: "When you see a fork in the road, take it."

Billy, Whitey, and the M&M Boys

Roger Maris and Mickey Mantle

"Everything looks nicer when you win. The girls are prettier. The cigars taste better. The trees are greener."

Billy Martin

A kiss from Phil Rizzuto probably wasn't one of the benefits of winning that Billy Martin had in mind, but he received a friendly peck from his infield teammate after Martin delivered the series-winning hit in the 1953 World Series against Brooklyn. Martin batted .500 in the six-game contest to help lead New York to its fifth consecutive championship. Over the years as a player and manager with the Yankees, Martin got to experience a lot of winning.

"You kind of took it for granted around the Yankees that there was always going to be baseball in October."

Whitey Ford, in his autobiography, Slick

And you could almost take it for granted that Whitey Ford would win some games in October, too. Ford appeared in 12 World Series with the Yankees, and no pitcher in history has won more series games than Ford (10). He also holds World Series records for most games started, most innings pitched, most strikeouts, most walks, most runs allowed, most hits allowed, and most games lost.

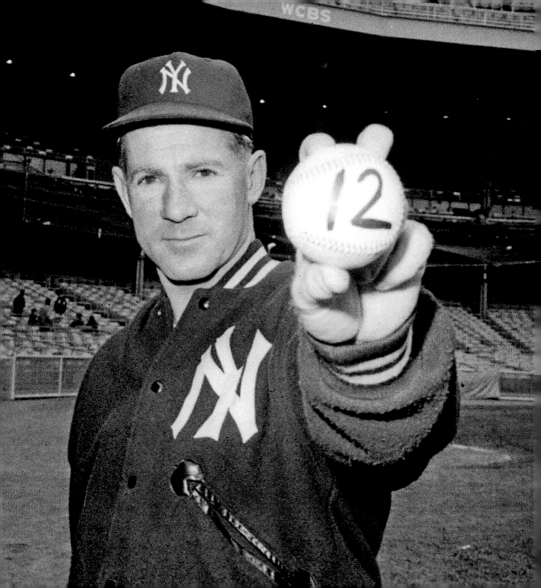

"I never threw the spitter. Well, maybe once or twice when I really needed to get a guy out real bad."

Whitey Ford

Ford was a tremendous competitor and always looked for that extra edge against the hitter. Spitballs and other "trick" pitches had been illegal in baseball for decades, but "Slick," as Ford was known, mastered several ways of doctoring a baseball. He would use his wedding ring or belt buckle to cut the ball and concocted a mixture of baby oil, turpentine, and resin for his famous "gunk ball."

"Hell, if I didn't drink or smoke, I'd win 20 games every year."

Whitey Ford

Ford enjoys a smoke alongside Billy Martin while practicing some putts before a golf tournament in Miami in 1958. Ford, Martin, and Mickey Mantle were an inseparable trio when they were Yankee teammates, especially in bars and nightclubs around New York City—although that didn't stop Ford from winning 236 games in his career, more than any Yankee in history. The carousing continued for Ford, Martin, and Mantle long after their playing days were over.

"Sooner or later, the arm goes bad. It has to. Sooner or later, you have to start pitching in pain."

Whitey Ford

In Ford's day, that philosophy was pretty much a given. Pitchers logged a lot of innings compared to today's hurlers. Ford's 283 innings pitched in 1961 has been topped by only three Yankee pitchers since (Ralph Terry, Mel Stottlemyre twice, and Catfish Hunter twice). After logging more than 244 innings in 1965 at the age of 36, Ford was used mostly as a reliever in 1966 and appeared in only seven games in 1967 before retiring.

"He's the best prospect I've ever seen."

Branch Rickey, on Mickey Mantle

That's high praise coming from Branch Rickey, one of the best executives and judges of talent in baseball history. As a fresh-faced 19-year-old in 1951, Mantle made an immediate impression on the league. He belted 19 homers in 96 games during his rookie season, and by his second season in 1952, he was batting over .300 and beginning a string of 14 consecutive all-star selections.

"He should lead the league in everything. With his combination of speed and power, he should win the triple crown every year. In fact, he should do anything he wants to do."

Casey Stengel, on Mickey Mantle

Casey Stengel was Mantle's first big-league manager, and he watched as the slugger emerged as the game's most dangerous hitter. The Mick did win a triple crown in 1956, when he led the American League with 52 home runs, 130 RBI, and a .353 average; he also was tops in runs scored and slugging percentage. Although he never won another batting title, Mantle batted over .300 ten times in his career and won four home run crowns.

"All I had was natural ability."

Mickey Mantle

Mickey Mantle was an excellent athlete, and he needed only one bat to do his damage at the plate. Like most athletes of the period, Mantle didn't believe in lifting weights or intense exercise regimens. Who knows how many home runs he would have hit if he had played in today's game, with the high-tech training equipment and superior sports medicine (not to mention performance-enhancing drugs).

"They ought to create a new league for that guy."

White Sox pitcher Jack Harshman, on Mickey Mantle

If "they" did create a new league, Mantle would probably have been the only guy in it. So Jack Harshman and the rest of the American League pitchers had no choice but to face Mantle during his 18-year career. Of course, they didn't always pitch to him. Mantle received more than 100 bases on balls in 10 different seasons. When he retired, only Babe Ruth and Ted Williams had more career free passes.

"Someone once asked me if I went up to the plate trying to hit a home run. Sure, every time."

Mickey Mantle

Well, not *every* time, as Mantle was known to lay down a bunt when the situation called for it. He also used his speed to take the extra base in ways other than sending the ball over the fence. In 1955, he led the league in triples, and in 1959 he stole 21 bases in 24 attempts. But, to be sure, he could send them deep, and Mantle had one of the highest home run ratios in baseball history.

"If I'd played my career hitting singles like Pete Rose, I'd wear a dress."

Mickey Mantle, in his autobiography, The Mick

Home run hitters tend to look down on singles hitters. Fellow slugger Ralph Kiner once famously quipped, "Home run hitters drive Cadillacs; singles hitters drive Fords." Nearly 1,500 of Mantle's 2,415 career hits were singles, but it was the 536 home runs that made the Mick an all-star, Hall of Famer, and baseball legend.

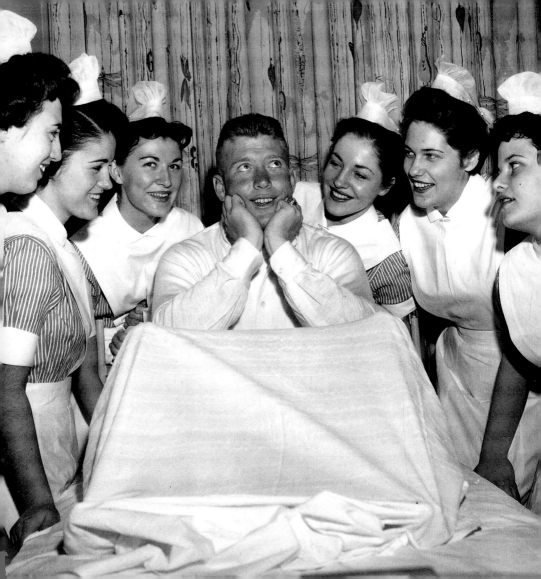

"Mantle's greatness was built on power and pain. He exuded the first and endured the second."

Ray Fitzgerald, Boston Globe *columnist*

Mantle seems to be enduring the pain well during this hospital visit in 1956. The Mick missed some 300 games over his career due to a variety of ailments—broken bones, knee problems, separated shoulders, torn hamstrings, to name a few—but he still endured through 18 major league seasons and played until he was 36 years old.

> ## "What can you say about Mickey after you say he was one of the greatest? He had talent he didn't realize he had."

Gene Woodling

Most people probably didn't know about Mantle's bowling talents, even teammate Gene Woodling, who played with Mantle from 1951 to 1954. Despite his gaudy career stats and Hall of Fame credentials, some felt that Mantle often took his own talents for granted. If he had been more focused on his health and not had such a raucous lifestyle, he might have accomplished even more.

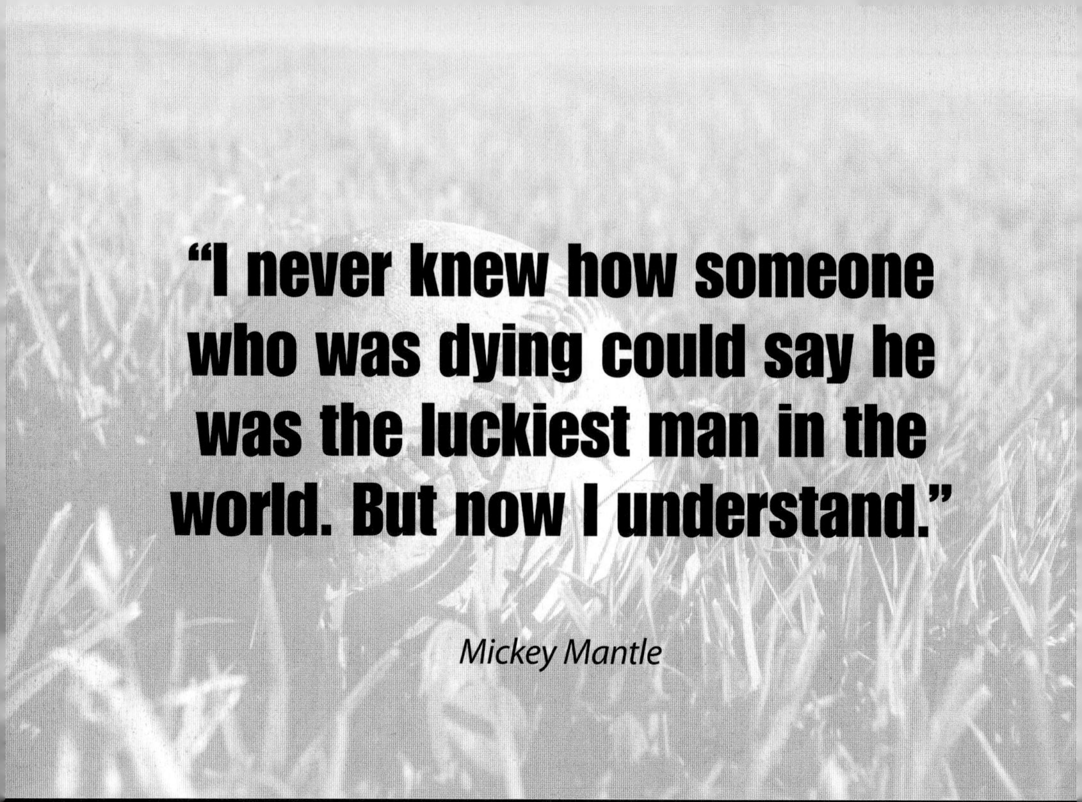

> # "I never knew how someone who was dying could say he was the luckiest man in the world. But now I understand."

Mickey Mantle

When Mantle's number 7 was retired by the Yankees on June 8, 1969, he invoked Lou Gehrig's immortal speech to illustrate what the Yankees and their fans meant to him. Pictured here with his wife and son, Mantle was a down-to-earth guy who didn't much like the spotlight and couldn't fully fathom why millions of fans adored him. By the end of his life, he was more appreciative of his fame.

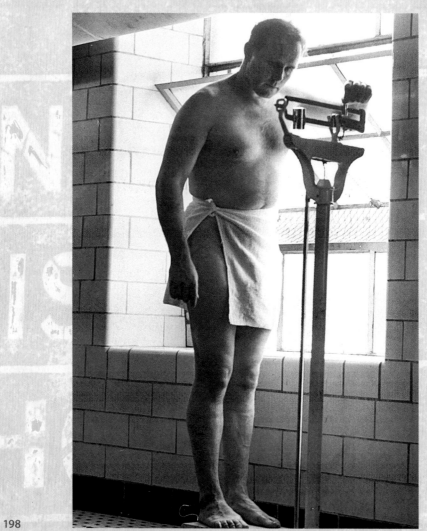

"If I knew I was going to live this long, I'd have taken better care of myself."

Mickey Mantle

Shown in the photo checking his weight during his playing days, Mantle offered a telling reflection on the life he lived not long before his death. According to those close to him, Mantle always believed that he would die young, like his father, Mutt, who worked for years in the hazardous conditions of the Oklahoma mines. Mantle lived to be 63 years old, when he died of liver cancer, in part caused by his years of heavy drinking.

"Sorry, Mickey, but because of the way you lived on earth, you can't come in. But before you leave, could you autograph some baseballs for Him?"

Mickey Mantle, on how St. Peter would greet him at the Pearly Gates

Mantle did not lead a virtuous life, and signing autographs was not one of his favorite activities. But here he obliges some eager young fans before an exhibition game between the Yankees and Senators in San Juan, Puerto Rico, during spring training in 1965.

"The best team lost."

Mickey Mantle

The scoreboard during Game Two of the 1960 World Series shows the Yankees leading Pittsburgh by a score of 15–1. They went on to win 16–3 and added romps of 10–0 and 12–0 in two other games. On paper, the Yankees simply dominated the Pirates during the series, outscoring them 55–27 in the seven games. But it all came down to one at bat, and Bill Mazeroski's dramatic series-winning homer for Pittsburgh in Game Seven was all they needed.

"Roger Maris was as good a man and as good a ballplayer as there ever was."

Mickey Mantle

Mickey Mantle and Roger Maris, the M&M Boys. As the two Yankee sluggers were in simultaneous pursuit of Babe Ruth's single-season home run record in 1961, many sportswriters tried to concoct a personal rivalry between the two. In reality, both men were too team-oriented to fall for that—they even roomed together in 1961.

"I don't want to be Babe Ruth. He was a great ballplayer. I'm not trying to replace him. The record is there, and damn right I want to break it, but that isn't replacing Babe Ruth."

Roger Maris

Just because Maris offers a kiss on the cheek to Mrs. Babe Ruth, don't get the wrong idea. As Maris' home run total mounted during the 1961 season, he felt increasing pressure and even hostility from fans and sportswriters for having the "audacity" to challenge the legacy of the great Ruth. Maris always insisted that he had no interest in usurping the Babe, only in hitting home runs, but that was not always recognized by outsiders.

"Two balls, no strikes on Roger Maris. Here's the windup. Fastball, hit deep to right! This could be it! Way back there! Holy cow, he did it! Sixty-one for Maris!"

Phil Rizzuto

Yankee broadcaster Phil Rizzuto made the call as Maris drove Tracy Stallard's pitch into the right field seats for home run number 61 in 1961. Rizzuto went on to comment on the fan frenzy to retrieve the historic ball, remarking, "Look at 'em fight for that ball out there!" Baseball collectibles was not as lucrative an enterprise as it is today, but everyone in the Yankee Stadium crowd that afternoon understood the significance of the moment—even though only 23,154 were in attendance.

> # "A season is a season, regardless of the number of games."

Joe Cronin

Joe Cronin, then the American League president, defended Maris' achievement after some sportswriters and other observers insisted that Ruth's home run total would have to be met within 154 games, the length of the 1927 season, in order to be legitimate. In the end, Maris needed all 162 games of the expanded 1961 schedule to catch Ruth, but despite the rumors, Maris' record was not branded with an asterisk. Maris did receive an MVP Award from Cronin.

"As a ballplayer, I would be delighted to do it again. As an individual, I doubt I could possibly go through it again."

Roger Maris

After hitting his 61st home run of the season in the final game, Maris reflected on what he went through chasing Ruth's record. Enduring intense scrutiny by the media all season long, the soft-spoken right fielder from Hibbing, Minnesota, was constantly being compared not only to Babe Ruth but also to friend and teammate Mickey Mantle. Mantle was a local hero and the preferred heir to the Babe. Maris' ability to persevere despite the pressure is a testament to his professionalism.

"You spend a good piece of your life gripping a baseball, and in the end it turns out that it was the other way around the whole time."

Jim Bouton

Jim Bouton helps fellow Yankee hurler Whitey Ford grip a baseball in this shot. Bouton spent close to a decade in the majors, but his best-known contribution to the baseball annals may have been his controversial book *Ball Four*, which offered an inside look at the life of a major leaguer and revealed insights into his former Yankee teammates.

"You can't get rich sitting on the bench, but it's worth a try."

Phil Linz

Phil Linz played for the Yankees from 1962 to 1965 as a backup infielder who spent a lot of time on the bench. He didn't get rich, but he did collect World Series shares in 1963 and 1964 and spent seven years in the big leagues.

"I like radio better than television because if you make a mistake on radio, they don't know. You can make up anything on the radio."

Phil Rizzuto

On the radio, they also can't see your funny hats, such as the one Rizzuto donned for a chilly game at Baltimore in April 1962. After 13 seasons as the Yankees' shortstop, Rizzuto made the switch to the broadcast booth, where he called Yankee games on both radio and television for 40 years. "Scooter" was known to make the occasional gaffe and even miss the action on the field. He was also an unabashed "homer."

"The older they get, the better they were when they were younger."

Jim Bouton, on Old Timers' Days

Old Timers' Days at Yankee Stadium could almost qualify as Hall of Fame reunion games, considering the legendary names that have played for the Yankees over the years. It's doubtful that Bouton received many invitations to such gatherings, but the 1974 roster included Hall of Famers Mickey Mantle, Yogi Berra, Whitey Ford, Joe DiMaggio, and Casey Stengel, among others.

> ## "When Elston Howard died, the Yankees lost more class than George Steinbrenner could buy in ten years."
>
> *Sportswriter Red Barber*

Elston Howard was indeed the epitome of class. He was the first African American to don the Yankee pinstripes at a time when blacks were still struggling for equal rights. Many of his family and friends believed that struggle was the reason he died at the young age of 51 in 1980. He was a nine-time all-star in 13 seasons with New York, and in 1963, he became the first African American to win the Most Valuable Player Award in the American League.

The
Bronx
Zoo

Fans run wild on the Yankee Stadium field after the Yankees won the 1978 World Series.

"Teamwork is playing together, which is necessary to win, whether it's hugging and kissing like the Dodgers or fighting and brawling like the Yankees."

Sparky Lyle, in The Bronx Zoo

Reggie Jackson gives Ron Guidry a big kiss following the Yankees' victory over the Los Angeles Dodgers in the 1978 World Series. With the volatile Billy Martin as manager and the cocky Jackson as the team's biggest star, the Yankees of the late 1970s did their fair share of fighting. Pitcher Sparky Lyle chronicled the experience in his best-selling book, *The Bronx Zoo*, which offered a behind-the-scenes look at the team during the 1978 season.

"Some kids dream of joining the circus, others of becoming a major league ballplayer. As a member of the New York Yankees, I've gotten to do both."

Graig Nettles

If the Yankees were a circus, then third baseman Graig Nettles was the high-wire act. He joined the team in 1973, the year that George Steinbrenner took over as principal owner. The all-star third baseman spent more than a decade with the club, helping to win four league pennants and two world championships—all while enduring Steinbrenner's meddling, squabbling, and at-times irrational behavior.

"I like hitting fourth and I like the good batting average. But what I do every day behind the plate is a lot more important."

Thurman Munson

Thurman Munson's importance to the Yankees between 1969 and 1979 was multifaceted indeed. Not only was he a consistent and clutch hitter who batted over .300 five times, he also was a standout defensive catcher and three-time Gold Glove Award winner; an expert at handling New York's pitching staff; and the first Yankee to be named team captain since Lou Gehrig. He was also a master at blocking the plate against opposing base runners, as he exhibits during the 1978 World Series.

"Thurman Munson was easy to umpire behind. He never held a grudge if I blew a call and was always a lot of fun to talk to, besides being a great catcher."

Umpire Ron Luciano

In addition to being popular among fans and teammates, Munson was respected and admired by the men in blue. If Munson argued a call, the umpires knew they probably blew it—although in this case, home plate umpire Fred Spenn didn't agree and ejected Munson from the game on July 15, 1979. Less than three weeks later, Munson was killed in a plane crash. It was a tragic loss not only for the Yankee organization, but for all of baseball.

> # "To be a Yankee is a thought in everyone's head. Just walking into Yankee Stadium, chills run through you."

Catfish Hunter

Jim "Catfish" Hunter seems pretty calm in this photo, taken just before his Yankee debut in April 1975. The previous December, Hunter signed with the team for a then-record contract worth $3.5 million. Coming off of a Cy Young Award season with Oakland, the expectations were high. He responded with 23 wins and a second-place finish in the Cy Young voting in 1975. A year later, his 17 wins helped the Yankees capture their first pennant in 12 years.

"If I had done everything I was supposed to have done, I'd be leading the league in homers, have the highest batting average, given $100,000 to the American Cancer Fund, and be married to Marie Osmond."

Catfish Hunter

For much of his career, Hunter did do nearly everything he was supposed to do. The eight-time all-star didn't miss a single start from 1965 until 1977. Then he began to suffer from arm problems and had to retire in 1979 at the age of 33. Among his many accomplishments, Hunter is the only pitcher ever to play for two different teams that won three straight pennants: the A's of 1972–1974 and the Yankees of 1976–1978.

"The sun don't shine on the same dog's ass all the time."

Catfish Hunter

It probably doesn't shine on the same elephant's ass either, but Hunter received this pachyderm as a gift upon his retirement in 1979. The North Carolina native—whose nickname "Catfish" was bestowed by Oakland A's owner Charlie Finley as a publicity ploy—adjusted to the circus-like atmosphere of the Yankees in the 1970s.

"If you're not having fun in baseball, you miss the point of everything."

Chris Chambliss

Yankee first baseman Chris Chambliss leaps for joy after knocking the game-winning home run in the clinching game of the American League Championship Series in 1976. Chambliss failed to make it all the way around the bases as thousands of fans stormed the Yankee Stadium field in celebration. Chambliss played first base on all three Yankee pennant winners from 1976 to 1978 and collected 90 or more RBI in each season.

"When I'm done managing, I'm going to open a kindergarten."

Billy Martin

Seen here in his playing days dressed as an angelic schoolboy, Billy Martin was an intense competitor as both a player and a manager. During his various tenures as Yankee skipper, Martin endured infighting among teammates and between himself and his players (most notably Reggie Jackson), and constant meddling and public criticism by his boss, George Steinbrenner. Martin probably often felt like a kindergarten teacher.

"It seems to me that the official rule book ought to be called the funny pages. The rule book is only good when you go deer hunting and run out of toilet paper."

Billy Martin

Martin was actually quite a student of the rule book and often used it to his advantage. He also never shied away from letting umpires know when he questioned their interpretation of the rules. The fiery manager was ejected from more than a few games in his 16 seasons as a major league skipper.

"All I know is, I pass people on the street, and they don't know whether I'm saying hello or goodbye."

Billy Martin

Martin, who had a tumultuous (to say the least) relationship with his boss, was fired and rehired by George Steinbrenner no fewer than four times and was threatened to be canned on countless other occasions. The fans always loved Billy, however, and he put the team back on the winning path.

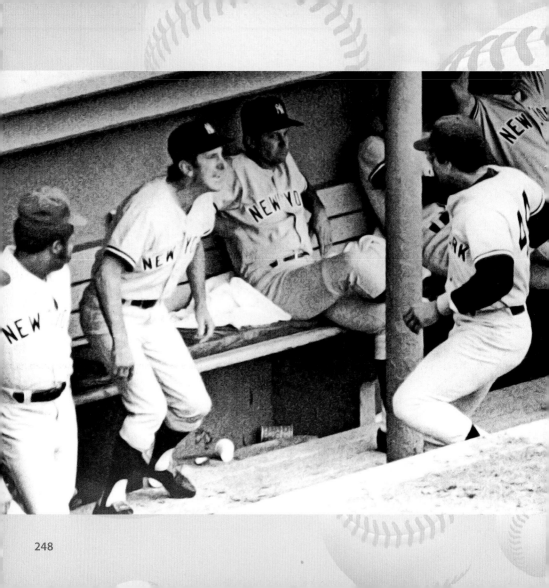

"Now there's a manager I could play for."

Reggie Jackson, on Billy Martin

Famous last words. Reggie Jackson said this while playing for Baltimore in 1976. After signing with the Yankees that offseason, the outspoken star frequently butted heads with his old-school manager. The feud hit its peak in July 1978 when, during a nationally televised game against Boston, Martin removed Jackson from his position in right field in the middle of an inning after Jackson lollygagged, in Martin's view, after a fly ball. When Jackson got to the dugout, the two engaged in a shouting match, and Martin had to be physically restrained.

"If I played in New York, they'd name a candy bar after me."

Reggie Jackson

And here it is: the Reggie! bar. On Opening Day 1978, every fan received a complimentary Reggie! candy bar. When Jackson hit a home run in the game, the fans showered the Yankee Stadium field with them. It was the last time the team gave away Reggie! bars.

REGGIE!®

NET WT. 1.5 OZ
(42 g)

Chocolaty covered caramel and peanuts

"When you open a Reggie! bar, it tells you how good it is."

Catfish Hunter

Jackson's self-confidence—some would say arrogance—often rubbed teammates the wrong way, and his outspokenness created tension in the Yankee clubhouse. Fortunately, the team persevered through the dissension and won back-to-back world championships in Jackson's first two seasons in New York.

"He'd give you the shirt off his back. Of course, he'd call a press conference to announce it."

Catfish Hunter, on Reggie Jackson

Few players knew Reggie like Catfish Hunter did. Hunter and Jackson were teammates for eight seasons with the Oakland A's and for four seasons in New York, so Hunter had seen and heard plenty of Jackson's shenanigans. And the Hall of Fame pitcher could dish out some pretty good one-liners.

"I didn't come here to be a star. I brought my star with me."

Reggie Jackson

When Jackson signed a contract worth nearly $3 million for five years—making him the highest paid Yankee and giving him plenty of money for fur coats—he was being paid for his star quality. He had played in six All-Star Games and won three championships as a member of the Oakland A's, and no less was expected of him in New York.

"I'm the straw that stirs the drink."

Reggie Jackson

Thurman Munson is not about to hit Jackson over the head with a bat in this photo from the 1978 World Series—but Jackson's quote, uttered during an interview with *Sport* magazine during spring training in 1977, definitely fostered tension between the two. Munson, the team captain and an all-star in his own right, bristled at the fact that Jackson made this statement before he had ever actually played a game in a Yankee uniform.

"One's a born liar, the other's convicted."

Billy Martin, on Reggie Jackson and George Steinbrenner

This comment by Martin was the final straw (for the first time) in his contentious relationships with the team's owner and star player. Martin was soon fired from the Yankees, 95 games into the 1978 season. Under his successor, Bob Lemon, the Yankees staged a historic late-season rally to win the pennant and the World Series. The liar and the criminal are pictured here at the press conference announcing that Jackson would don a Yankees cap on his plaque in Cooperstown.

"Fans don't boo nobodies."

Reggie Jackson

Jackson received plenty of both cheers and boos during his Hall of Fame career. Beloved when he was belting homers and driving in runs, Jackson was harshly criticized by fans and the media whenever he slumped. His boastful proclamations and high salary meant that people had little patience for sub-par performances. When he hit three home runs in Game Six of the 1977 World Series, however, he earned nothing but cheers from the Yankee Stadium crowd.

"There isn't enough mustard in the world to cover that hot dog."

Darold Knowles, on Reggie Jackson

Relief pitcher Darold Knowles was Jackson's teammate on three championship teams in Oakland during the early 1970s, and even then Jackson's ego was renown. Not that he hadn't earned it. By the time he came to New York in 1977, Jackson had captured an American League MVP Award (1973), a World Series MVP (also in 1973, and which earned him this car), and six All-Star Game appearances.

"No wonder you're all mixed up. You got a white man's first name, a Spanish man's second name, and a black man's third name."

Mickey Rivers, to Reginald Martinez Jackson

Mickey Rivers was Reggie Jackson's teammate for three seasons, and "Mick the Quick" was often a font of colorful quotes. The down-to-earth Rivers was easily overshadowed by his celebrated teammates in media-saturated New York, but he was always quick with a quip—and on the base paths.

"Better stop readin' and writin', and start hittin'."

Mickey Rivers, to Reggie Jackson

Rivers was ready with a retort after Jackson declared, in front of several reporters, that Rivers could not read or write. While Rivers didn't seem particularly bright, he was always able to torment his flashy, college-educated teammate. Here Jackson relaxes in his Manhattan apartment overlooking Central Park.

"After I hit a home run, I had a habit of running the bases with my head down. I figure the pitcher already felt bad enough without me showing him up rounding the bases."

Mickey Mantle

Reggie Jackson didn't quite share Mantle's sympathy for opposing pitchers. Jackson mastered the art of admiring his own achievements while standing at home plate. Of course, in Mantle's day, batters who showed up pitchers usually got a fastball to the ribs the next time they stepped in the batter's box.

"I don't care how long you've been around, you'll never see it all."

Bob Lemon

In more than 40 years as a pitcher, coach, and manager, Bob Lemon saw a lot, but his time in New York was full of surprises. He was hired to replace Billy Martin as Yankee manager midway through the 1978 season and led the team to a World Series victory. Lemon was then fired 65 games into the 1979 season to make room for Martin's return. Lemon was rehired in 1981 and again carried the Yanks to a pennant, then was fired 14 games into the 1982 season.

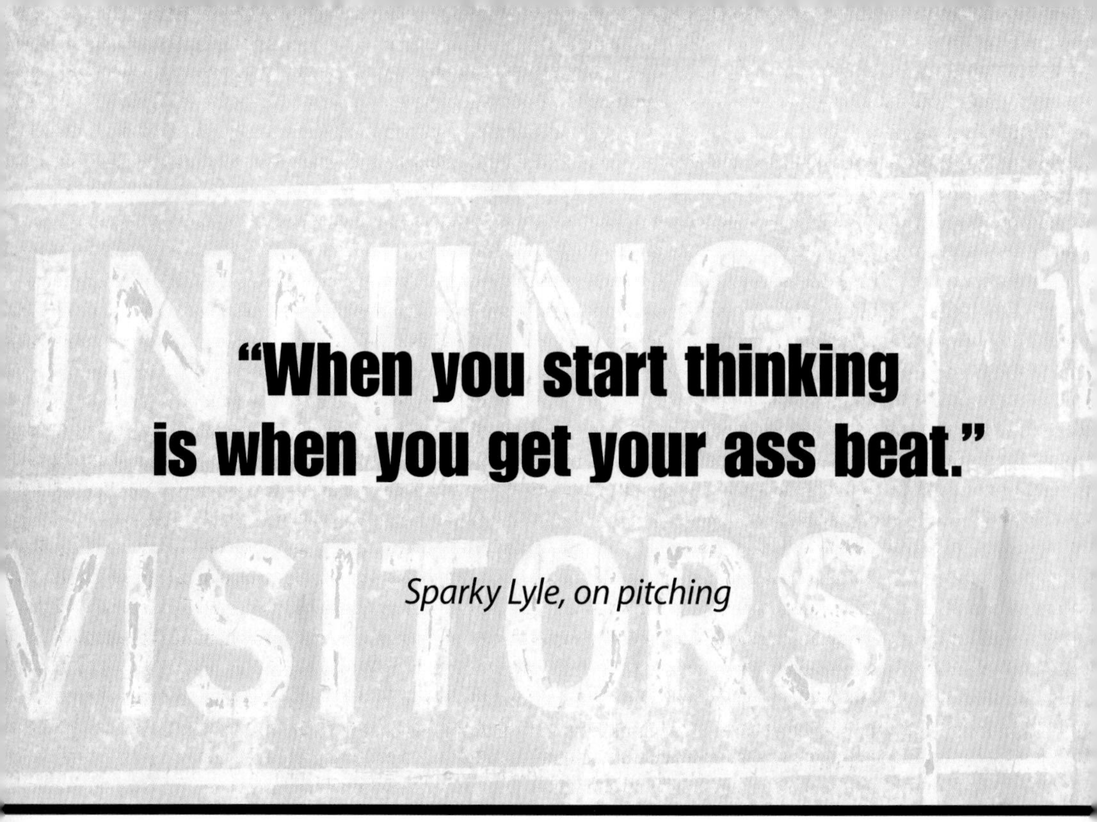

"When you start thinking is when you get your ass beat."

Sparky Lyle, on pitching

Sparky Lyle—shown here displaying his award for Life Saver of the Month in June 1973—didn't get his ass beat very often. When he retired in 1982 with 238 career saves, he ranked third on the all-time saves list. Lyle wasn't afraid to think either, and his tell-all book, *The Bronx Zoo*, revealed a lot about the game of baseball and about the New York Yankees.

"Why pitch nine innings when you can get just as famous pitching two?"

Sparky Lyle, on being a relief pitcher

Lyle's fame increased in 1977 when he became the first relief pitcher from the American League to win the Cy Young Award, on the heels of his 13–5 record, 2.17 ERA, and 26 saves. He pitched in 72 games that season and threw only 137 innings, an average of less than two innings per appearance. He is shown here with his wife after he received the award.

"He's gone from Cy Young to sayonara."

Graig Nettles, on Sparky Lyle

When the Yankees acquired star closer Goose Gossage in 1978, Lyle was relegated to setup man—a role he despised—and his saves total dropped from 26 in 1977 to 9 in 1978. He spent the whole season hoping to be traded and aired a lot of dirty laundry in *The Bronx Zoo*. In November 1978, Lyle got his wish and was traded to Texas—where he saved 13 games in 1979.

> **"There's smoke coming out of his nose and his cap is down over his eyes, and he's so big and hulking. You need a cape to face Gossage, not a baseball bat."**
>
> *Tom Paciorek*

The 6-foot-3 Rich "Goose" Gossage had a blazing fastball and an intimidating presence on the mound. In 1978, he saved a league-leading 27 games and helped carry New York to a world championship. Gossage was never enamored with the circus-like atmosphere of Steinbrenner's Yankees, but during his six seasons with the team (1978–1983), he was one of the most dominating relievers the game has ever seen.

"If this club wants somebody to play third base, they've got me. If they want somebody to go to luncheons, they should hire Georgie Jessel."

Graig Nettles

Graig Nettles and several other Yankees were fined by George Steinbrenner after failing to attend a mandatory team luncheon. A few days after Nettles made this comment, he received a card from George Jessel, a comedic actor and popular emcee at gatherings. The card read, "Thanks for getting me in the newspapers." Nettles himself was in the newspapers frequently for his acrobatic fielding plays.

"Well, that kind of puts a damper on even a Yankee win."

Phil Rizzuto, on the death of Pope Paul VI

As a lifelong Yankee, first as a player and then as a broadcaster, it's perhaps understandable that the fortunes of the baseball team were foremost in Phil Rizzuto's mind, even after hearing of the death of the pope in 1978. He wasn't trying to be funny or flip, but the "Scooter" received criticism for his comment. Here, Rizzuto stands amidst the construction equipment during the Yankee Stadium renovation in 1974, which really put a damper on things for Yankee fans.

"My goals are to hit .300, score 100 runs, and stay injury-prone."

Mickey Rivers

Mickey Rivers was somewhat clear about his goals heading into his first season with the Yankees, and he met most of those benchmarks. He batted .312, scored 95 runs, and missed 25 games, which was the most "injury-prone" he would be in his three years in New York.

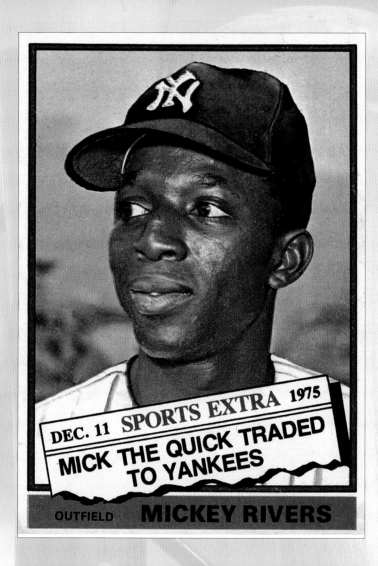

DEC. 11 SPORTS EXTRA 1975

MICK THE QUICK TRADED TO YANKEES

OUTFIELD **MICKEY RIVERS**

287

"I take my old lady dancing every night now. Doing 'The Bump' keeps your legs in shape."

Mickey Rivers

The 1970s dance craze known as "the Bump" probably wasn't on most players' training regimes, but it worked for Rivers. In his first season in New York in 1977, he stole 43 bases while being caught only 7 times, and his runs total jumped from 70 to 95 as the Yankees' leadoff man. Here, he uses some fancy footwork to get an infield hit in 1977.

"Me and George and Bill are two of a kind."

Mickey Rivers, on George Steinbrenner and Billy Martin

Rivers (second from left) stands next to his manager before Game Three of the 1977 World Series. Also pictured are (from left) Willie Randolph, Thurman Munson, and Reggie Jackson. Rivers could bunt, steal, and hit with some power, although he also had nearly twice as many strikeouts as walks in his career—not a great quality in a leadoff man.

291

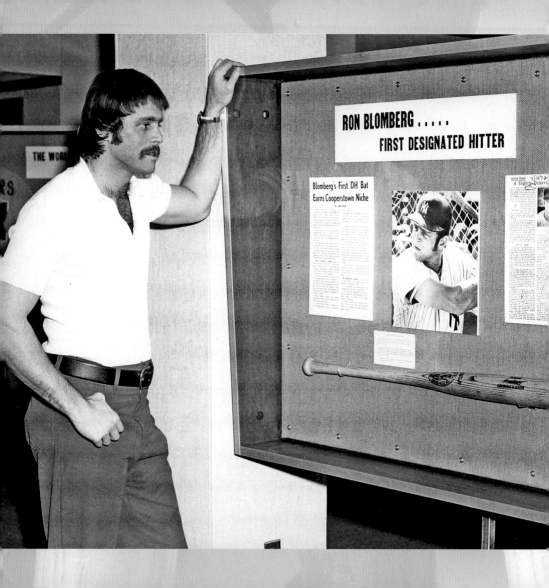

RON BLOMBERG . . . . .
FIRST DESIGNATED HITTER

Blomberg's First DH Bat
Earns Cooperstown Niche

"I got into the Hall of Fame through the back door."

Ron Blomberg

A lifetime .293 hitter in 461 major league games, Ron Blomberg didn't earn a display in the Hall of Fame for his skills as a ballplayer. He got there for being the game's first designated hitter after the rule was instituted in the American League for the 1973 season. Blomberg presumably came in through the front door of the Hall of Fame to pose for this photo.

"You dream about things like that when you're a kid. Well, my dream came true."

Bucky Dent

Bucky Dent's three-run, seventh-inning home run was the turning point in the one-game playoff between the Yankees and Red Sox on October 2, 1978, to determine the East Division title. The light-hitting shortstop capped off a frenzied comeback season for the Yankees, who rallied from 14 games back to catch and ultimately defeat the rival Red Sox. It was the career highlight for Dent, a .247 hitter with 40 lifetime home runs.

King
George

George Steinbrenner, looking regal

"I won't be active in the day-to-day operations of the club at all."

George Steinbrenner

In one of his first press conferences after purchasing the New York Yankees in 1973, George Steinbrenner let it be known that he planned to be an absentee owner of the team. It wasn't long before Steinbrenner was offering his two cents on nearly every baseball decision. At times openly critical of the team, "the Boss" occasionally created dissension and instability in the clubhouse, and managers and players were put on edge by his constant meddling.

"Winning is the most important thing in my life, after breathing. Breathing first, winning second."

George Steinbrenner

Say what you will about Steinbrenner and his ownership style, but he did restore winning ways to the Bronx. Within the first six seasons under Steinbrenner, the Yankees won three pennants and two world championships. Following a 15-year hiatus from the Fall Classic, the team returned to the top in the late 1990s, winning four titles between 1996 and 2000 under manager Joe Torre. Owner and manager shared an emotional moment after winning the 1998 World Series.

"I am dead set against free agency. It can ruin baseball."

George Steinbrenner

Probably no individual in baseball did more to advance the proliferation of free agency than the Yankees owner. As one of the top revenue-producing clubs in sports, the Yankees spent freely on several high-profile players within the first few years of free agency. Some of them worked out well for Steinbrenner and the Yankees, such as Catfish Hunter, Reggie Jackson, and Rich Gossage. Others proved to be expensive failures—Ed Whitson comes to mind.

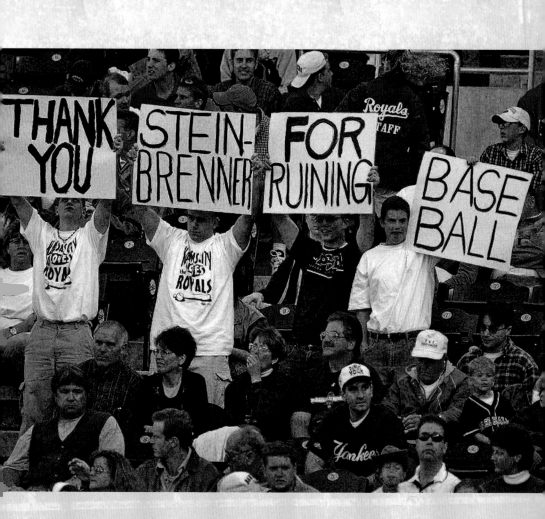

"Every time we make trouble, ol' George flies out here from another part of the country and gets in our way. Maybe we should make a lot of trouble, so he'll keep flying out here. Sooner or later, his plane's gonna crash."

Dock Ellis

Dock Ellis was 17–8 with a 3.19 ERA for the Yankees in 1976. He made the above comment during spring training prior to the 1977 season. On April 27 of that year, Ellis was traded to the Oakland A's, despite posting a 1.83 ERA for New York in his first three starts. The moral of the story: Don't mess with George.

"Why shouldn't I speak out? Don't you speak out in this country?"

George Steinbrenner

Steinbrenner was uncharacteristically tight-lipped upon leaving Commissioner Fay Vincent's office in July 1990. The baseball commissioner banned Steinbrenner from baseball for his dealings with a gambler named Howie Spira and trying to discredit Yankees star Dave Winfield. Steinbrenner was reinstated in 1993, and his involvement in the day-to-day operations of the team was more muted—although that didn't stop him from speaking out when the spirit moved him.

"I was often misquoted. I was supportive of my managers, even though they all may not think so."

George Steinbrenner

Steinbrenner was generally supportive of his managers when they were winning, but once they started losing, no one was safe. He fired Billy Martin in August 1978, after Martin led the Yankees to their first title in 16 years in 1977. In his first 20 seasons owning the team, Steinbrenner made 20 managerial changes involving 13 different managers.

"Owning the Yankees is like owning the Mona Lisa."

George Steinbrenner

It is difficult to gauge the value of a unique piece of artwork, but some estimate the value of the Mona Lisa to be between $500 million and $1 billion. According to a *Forbes* magazine report, the New York Yankees franchise was worth approximately $1.3 billion in 2008. Steinbrenner purchased the team for $10 million in 1973. Not a bad investment for old George. Here he admires the artist's rendering of New Yankee Stadium, with Mayor Michael Bloomberg and Governor George Pataki.

CHEREPAK · ATZENWEILER

Modern
Times

Yankee Stadium, alive with action

"I'm glad I don't have to face him every day. He has that look that few hitters have."

Dwight Gooden, on Don Mattingly

In each of his first three full major league seasons (1984–1986), Don Mattingly had 200 or more hits, 40 or more doubles, at least 110 RBI, and batted higher than .320. More than just a fearsome hitter, he was virtually flawless in the field and claimed nine Gold Glove Awards in 10 seasons. Mattingly's one great career shortcoming was never appearing in a World Series.

"If my uniform doesn't get dirty, I haven't done anything in the baseball game."

Rickey Henderson

Sporting a dirty uniform during the 1987 season, Rickey Henderson accomplished plenty in his time with the Yankees. He is the all-time franchise leader in stolen bases, led the league in thefts in all but one season while playing for the Yankees, and was voted as a starter in the All-Star Game every year he wore a Yankee uniform.

"This s--- don't count. This s--- don't go on the back of the bubblegum card."

Rickey Henderson, on spring training

Ricky Henderson was eccentric—some might say downright weird. But the man loved to play baseball, and play it well. He spent 25 years in the majors with nine different teams, spending the most time with the A's and Yankees. He is baseball's all-time leader in stolen bases and runs scored, and he holds the single-season stolen base record—all in games that counted.

"All I ever wanted was to be a Yankee."

Derek Jeter

Selected by the Yankees with the sixth overall pick in the 1992 amateur draft, Derek Jeter signed with the team on June 27, 1992, the day after his 18th birthday. Jeter (left) visited with Jim Leyritz and Mike Gallego at Yankee Stadium that September, and he's been a fixture in pinstripes ever since. Barring injury or a trade, by 2011 Jeter will pass Mickey Mantle as the all-time leader in games played with the New York Yankees.

"My dad had been a shortstop when he was in college, and you know, when you're a kid, you want to be just like your dad."

Derek Jeter

Jeter has played all but 11 of his 1,969 games at shortstop (through 2008) and has played more games at the position than anyone else in Yankee history. He's also earned nine all-star selections at shortstop, five as the starter. He won three consecutive Gold Glove Awards (2004–2006) and the Silver Slugger Award in 2006 and 2007.

"If you're going to play at all, you've got to win."

Derek Jeter

Jeter has done plenty of winning in his first 14 seasons with New York. Through 2008, he has played in an astonishing 25 postseason series, including 12 Divisional Series, 7 American League Championship Series, and 6 World Series. Jeter and the Yankees are 17–8 in those series. Jeter played on four world champions by the time he was 27 years old.

"You gotta have fun. Regardless of how you look at it, we're playing a game. It's a business, it's our job, but I don't think you can do well unless you're having fun."

Derek Jeter

As a leader on the field and in the clubhouse, Jeter always seems to be having fun. He's also done his job about as well as anyone in the league. Jeter has been among the top 10 batting leaders in 8 of his 14 seasons, collected at least 200 hits in a season six times, and is on pace to become the first Yankee in history to join the 3,000-hit club. He's shown here having fun with manager Joe Girardi in 2008.

"In big games, the action slows down for him where it speeds up for others. I've told him, I'll trade my past for your future."

Reggie Jackson, on Derek Jeter

Jeter has only four World Series rings to Jackson's five, although "Mr. October" didn't play in the 1972 series, when Oakland beat the Reds, because of a leg injury. Jeter—who earned the nickname "Mr. November" during the 2001 World Series for his Game Four heroics, which concluded in extra innings on November 1—has a .302 lifetime average and 27 runs scored in 32 World Series games.

"He's a hunk.
And I don't even like that word."

Actress Kim Basinger, on Derek Jeter

Jeter is popular with females of all ages. And he's not just a pretty face. Good looks and rich, too. According to *Forbes* magazine, Jeter raked in $7 million in endorsements alone in 2007, to go along with his $21.6 million salary. Of course, he wasn't even the highest paid player on his own team, trailing both Alex Rodriguez and Jason Giambi.

"Hanging out with him sucks. All the women flock to him."

Tim Raines, on Derek Jeter

Women even flock to him in the middle of games, as in this scene from 2002 at Yankee Stadium. Jeter has been linked romantically to a bevy of beauties, including Mariah Carey, former Miss Universe Lara Dutta, and actress Jessica Biel, among many others. Although teammate A-Rod got in some hot water for his relationship with Madonna in 2008, Jeter's dalliances apparently haven't been a distraction.

"With this club, it doesn't matter where you hit. You're going to have people on base one through nine."

Bernie Williams, in 1996

The 1996 Yankees secured the team's first pennant in 15 years and the first World Series triumph in 18 years. At the heart of the lineup was center fielder Bernie Williams (number 51), one of five regulars to bat over .300 for the season. A lifelong Yankee, Williams batted over .300 in eight consecutive seasons and led the league with a .339 mark in 1998.

"You play the game to win the game, not to worry about what's on back of the baseball card."

Paul O'Neill

The selfless but fiercely competitive Paul O'Neill always played to win, often wearing his emotions on his sleeve. He wasn't the flashiest Yankee, but the back of O'Neill's baseball card would reveal that during his time in New York, he was selected to four all-star teams, won a batting title in 1994, and hit .303 over the nine seasons. Oh, and the team won nearly 60 percent of the time.

"We don't have a big guy. We have a team full of big guys."

Tim Raines, on the 1998 Yankees

The 1998 Yankees won 114 regular season games and finished 22 games ahead of the second-place Red Sox. They led the American League in most runs scored and fewest runs allowed. While Bernie Williams, Derek Jeter, Scott Brosius, Paul O'Neill, and David Wells were named to the all-star team, the veteran Tim Raines chipped in with a .290 average and 53 runs on the season.

"You don't win 114 games by being lucky."

Mike Hargrove, on the 1998 Yankees

Cleveland manager Mike Hargrove (left) got a quick lesson in luck from Joe Torre at the 1998 American League Championship Series. Actually, Hargrove's Indians were the only team to get a jump on Torre's Yankees in the postseason. After taking a two-games-to-one lead in the series, Cleveland lost the next three to give New York the pennant. The Yanks went on to sweep the San Diego Padres in the World Series.

"When you go to other parks, they hang banners for the Wild Card, or the Eastern Division or Western Division champions. Around here, they don't hang anything unless it's for being world champions."

Chili Davis

Veteran Chili Davis gets blasted with champagne by teammates after the Yankees clinched the 1999 Eastern Division title, but the real celebrations were still to come. After winning 98 games during the regular season, the Yanks went 11–1 in the postseason and won a second straight World Series. It was Davis' final season in the majors, but the 39-year-old designated hitter played 146 games for the world champions.

TEAM OF THE CENTURY
WORLD CHAMPIONSHIP TROPHY
PRESENTED BY THE COMMISSIONER OF BASEBALL

"If you're a Yankee fan or not a Yankee fan, you have to admit, we're winners."

Paul O'Neill

Right fielder Paul O'Neill was one of four everyday starters to play on all four Yankee championship teams between 1996 and 2000; the others were first baseman Tino Martinez, shortstop Derek Jeter, and center fielder Bernie Williams. After the franchise won its 25th World Series title in 1999, manager Joe Torre, New York Mayor Rudy Guiliani, and owner George Steinbrenner celebrated the Yankees' place as the "Team of the Century."

"I am not perfect."

Mariano Rivera

Mariano Rivera may not be perfect, but since the late 1990s he's been about as close as anyone in the majors. Arguably the greatest relief pitcher of all time, he has led the American League in saves three times and finished in the top 10 in every season since becoming the Yankees' closer in 1997. Nearly unstoppable in October, Rivera has an ERA of 0.77 in 76 career postseason games (through 2008), and he won the World Series MVP Award in 1999.

"Everybody kind of perceives me as being angry. It's not anger, it's motivation."

Roger Clemens

Roger Clemens sure appeared angry when he picked up the remnants of Mike Piazza's broken bat during Game Two of the 2000 World Series and hurled it in Piazza's general direction. The pitcher claimed that he was simply throwing the bat off the field of play, but Piazza was none too pleased, and words were exchanged. Nevertheless, Clemens was motivated enough to win the game and put the Yanks on the path to another championship.

"The only stage I need is the World Series."

Alex Rodriguez

Alex Rodriguez's individual accomplishments place him among the all-time greats: three MVP Awards, five home run crowns, a batting title, two Gold Gloves, and more than 500 career home runs, all accomplished by the time A-Rod was 32 years old. Ironically, as of 2008, the Yankees have not made it to the World Series since acquiring the future Hall of Famer.

"Waking up at six in the morning! There's been many nights when I haven't gotten to bed at six in the morning."

Johnny Damon, on Alex Rodriguez's workout schedule

In addition to being a night owl in his time with the Red Sox, Johnny Damon also let his hair and beard grow long, and he proudly proclaimed himself as one of the crew of "idiots" that won the 2004 title in Boston. When Damon became a teammate of A-Rod's with the Yankees in 2006, he cleaned up his act a bit—at least as far as his grooming is concerned. Whether there's been a change in his after-hours lifestyle is not as apparent.

"The National League needs to join the twenty-first century. They need to grow up."

Hank Steinbrenner, on the designated hitter rule

Hank Steinbrenner, who took over for his father as the Yankees' new boss in 2008, was incensed after Yankee pitcher Chien-Ming Wang was injured running the bases during an interleague game. While it's unlikely that the younger Steinbrenner is going to bring about a change in a 35-year-old rule in the National League, it's clear that Hank Steinbrenner is nearly as combative as his dad.

"If we sign him, he's 28. If he signs somewhere else, he's 48."

General Manager Brian Cashman,
on Orlando Hernandez

There was a lot of controversy surrounding the true age of Cuban exile Orlando Hernandez before the Yankees signed him in 1998. Regardless of his age, "El Duque" showed youthful exuberance in posting a 12–4 record and 3.13 ERA in his rookie season, while helping the Yankees to a World Series victory. (Most sources cite his birthday as October 11, 1965, which means he was 32 years old when he made his Yankee debut.)

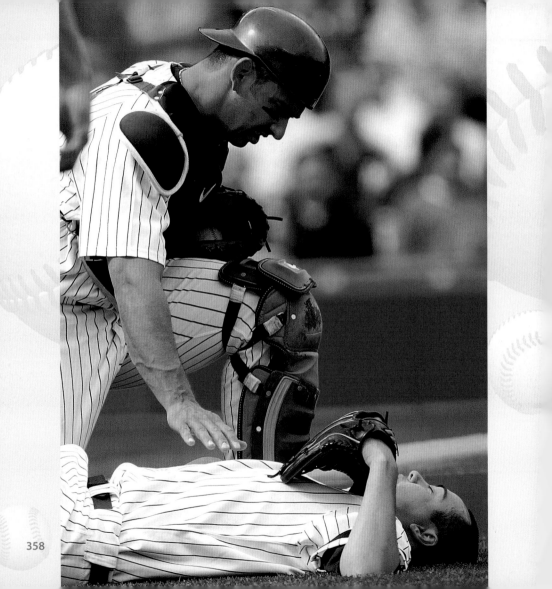

"Sometimes the hitter gets a hit, sometimes I strike them out, but in neither case does anyone die."

Orlando Hernandez

Catcher Jorge Posada isn't applying last rites to pitcher Jeff Karstens—Karstens was just grounded by a line drive during a game in April 2007. Orlando Hernandez has put some batters on their backs as well during his career. Among active pitchers, "El Duque" boasts one of the lowest ratios of hits allowed per nine innings, and his strikeouts per nine innings ranks better than many other star hurlers, including Andy Pettitte and Mike Mussina.

"I hope his co-workers kicked the s--- out of him."

Hank Steinbrenner

The younger Steinbrenner had no kind words for the construction worker who buried a David Ortiz Red Sox jersey in the foundation of the New Yankee Stadium during construction in April 2008. The Yankees had the concrete dug up and the shirt removed, and according to several news sources, nobody kicked the s--- out of anyone. Although the worker did get fired.

The
Stadium

Yankee Stadium, 1972

"Yankee Stadium was a mistake. Not mine, but the Giants'."

Yankees owner Jacob Ruppert

From 1913 to 1922, the Yankees played their home games at the Polo Grounds as tenants of the New York Giants. When they started drawing larger crowds than the Giants, the landlords raised the rent in the hopes of forcing the team to an outer borough. Jacob Ruppert and his Yankees had the last laugh. In April 1923, they opened a lavish new stadium in the Bronx, directly across the Harlem River from the Polo Grounds.

"Some ballyard!"

Babe Ruth, on Yankee Stadium

Some ballyard, indeed. Babe Ruth loved the inviting right field porch, into which he planted many of his homers while playing for the Yankees, and that part of the Stadium was called "Ruthville" in his honor for as long as he played there. Ruth had established himself as a veritable superstar by the time the Stadium opened in 1923, and the ballpark was bestowed with the nickname "the House That Ruth Built."

> # "When I first came to Yankee Stadium, I used to feel like the ghosts of Babe Ruth and Lou Gehrig were walking around in there."

Mickey Mantle

No ghosts were sighted, but monuments honoring Ruth, Gehrig, and manager Miller Huggins were installed at the original Yankee Stadium, and before the 1974 renovation, they were located on the field of play. Mickey Mantle was the fourth Yankee to receive a monument, and Joe DiMaggio was so honored after his death in 1999. Twenty other former Yankee players, executives, or broadcasters are celebrated with plaques at Yankee Stadium's Monument Park.

GEORGE HERMAN "BABE" RUTH
1895 - 1948

A GREAT BALL PLAYER
A GREAT MAN
A GREAT AMERICAN

ERECTED BY
THE YANKEES
AND
THE NEW YORK BASEBALL WRITERS

APRIL 19, 1949

"The Stadium was like the Grand Canyon or Empire State Building of baseball. Every time I stepped inside it, I had to pinch myself."

Yankee broadcaster Mel Allen

Mel Allen stepped into Yankee Stadium many times during his long career as a broadcaster. He was the voice of the Yankees from 1940 to 1963 (missing several years due to World War II). He was fired in 1964 but returned to the Yankee broadcast booth in 1976. The Hall of Fame broadcaster called many historic moments at Yankee Stadium, including 14 World Series.

"Yankee Stadium is my favorite stadium. I'm not going to lie to you. There's a certain feel you get in Yankee Stadium."

Derek Jeter

Jeter has plenty of reasons to favor Yankee Stadium. His career average is .322 at home compared to .310 on the road, and in September 2008, he broke the all-time record for most career hits at the original Yankee Stadium, passing Lou Gehrig. Jeter and the rest of the Yankee faithful hope that the tradition continues in the New Yankee Stadium, which opened in 2009.

"I thought it would be in black and white."

Greg Maddux, on his first visit to Yankee Stadium

Greg Maddux, a virtual lock for the Hall of Fame, was a 10-year major league veteran and four-time Cy Young Award winner before he played his first game at Yankee Stadium. His debut came in Game Two of the 1996 World Series, and he sapped the color out of the Yankee lineup, pitching a shutout victory, although he lost the sixth and final game of that series at the Stadium.

"People from out of town say there are three things they want to see: the Statue of Liberty, Radio City, and Yankee Stadium."

Bill Waite, longtime Yankee Stadium employee

New York City has no shortage of tourist attractions, and to be sure, Yankee Stadium is always a popular destination for visitors and locals alike. From 1923 to 2008, the Stadium was the American League attendance leader 44 times, including a stretch of 11 seasons in a row (1949–1959). In 1946, the Yankees became the first team to draw two million fans in a season.

"Why do people sing 'Take Me Out to the Ballgame' when they're already there?"

Alex Rodriguez

A-Rod asks a good question. But the apparent lack of logic behind the song's tradition doesn't stop more than 50,000 fans at Yankee Stadium from rising to their feet every game during the seventh inning and joining in a rousing rendition of the classic baseball ditty.

"The Yankees were not our team. They were our religion."

Jerry Coleman

For decades, Yankee Stadium has been an almost-holy site for baseball players and fans alike. The original stadium hosted three holy visits in its history, welcoming three different Catholic popes. Pope Paul VI gave a Mass to more than 90,000 spectators in October 1965, and Pope John Paul II came in 1979. Most recently, Pope Benedict XVI celebrated Mass in front of a capacity crowd in April 2008.

Opposing
Views

Boston's Jason Varitek vs. Alex Rodriguez, 2004

> "The majority of American males put themselves to sleep by striking out the batting order of the New York Yankees."

James Thurber

Not many pitchers could strike out the 1936 Yankee batting order, which was one of the fiercest lineups in baseball history. Thurber, a popular humorist and essayist, first moved to New York in 1925 and joined the staff of *The New Yorker* in 1927. He died in 1961, and his career coincided almost exactly with the greatest period of the Yankee dynasty.

"I would rather beat the Yankees regularly than pitch a no-hit game."

Bob Feller

Bob Feller, a Hall of Fame pitcher for the Cleveland Indians, was able to accomplish both on April 30, 1946, when he defeated New York in a 1–0 no-hitter at Yankee Stadium. Feller's Indians were also the only team to displace the Yankee dynasty from atop the American League between 1947 and 1958. Cleveland won pennants in 1948 and 1954 in the midst of New York's run of 10 pennants in 12 seasons.

"Rooting for the Yankees is like rooting for U.S. Steel."

Comedian Joe E. Lewis

This famous quip (which has been attributed to several sources) encapsulates the way that much of America views the Yankee monolith. With more championships than any other professional sports franchise, not to mention a long roster of Hall of Famers and baseball pioneers, the Yankees have been the dominant force in the game for more than six decades—nearly as long as U.S. Steel's dominance of American industry—and millions come out every year to root them on.

"Bucky F---ing Dent."

Don Zimmer

Boston manager Don Zimmer effectively summed up the Red Sox Nation's view of Bucky Dent's historic home run off Mike Torrez in the 1978 playoff—and that's how Dent is still known throughout New England. Contrary to popular legend, Dent's homer didn't win the game for the Yankees, but only gave them the lead. Reggie Jackson's lead-off homer against Bob Stanley in the eighth proved to be the winning margin. But Dent's blast was the killer.

"The Evil Empire extends its tentacles even into Latin America."

Larry Lucchino, after the Yankees signed pitcher Jose Contreras in 2002

Boston Red Sox president Larry Lucchino labeled the Yankees with the "Evil Empire" moniker in 2002 after New York signed the coveted Cuban pitcher Jose Contreras. Few teams suffered more at the hands of the Yankees than the Red Sox, and the "Curse of the Bambino" haunted the Red Sox Nation for decades. Boston has had the upper hand in recent years, however, capturing world titles in 2004 and 2007 and defeating them in the 2004 League Championship Series.

"What can I say?
The Yankees are my daddy."

Pedro Martinez

All-star Red Sox hurler Pedro Martinez uttered these words after losing a disappointing game to the Yankees late in the 2004 season. It was more a statement made in frustration than an acknowledgment of any inherent superiority on the part of the Yankees—and Boston ultimately defeated New York in the playoffs and won the World Series that year—but Martinez has been taunted with the "Who's your daddy" chant in ballparks around the country ever since.

1978 NEW YORK YANKEES

First Row Seated — THURMAN MUNSON, ELSTON HOWARD, DICK HOWSER, BOB LEMON, YOGI BERRA, ART FOWLER, CLYDE KING, GENE MICHAEL, GARY THOMASSON, ROY WHITE, ED FIGUEROA.

Second Row — GENE MONAHAN (TRAINER), DOM SCALA (BULLPEN CATCHER), BRIAN DOYLE, BUCKY DENT, RON GUIDRY, KEN CLAY, LARRY McCALL, JIM BEATTIE, RICH GOSSAGE, DICK TIDROW, LOU PINIELLA, FRED STANLEY, HERMAN SCHNEIDER (TRAINER), PETE SHEEHY (EQUIP-MENT MANAGER).

Back Row — REGGIE JACKSON, CLIFF JOHNSON, JAY JOHNSTONE, WILLIE RANDOLPH, CATFISH HUNTER, CHRIS CHAMBLISS, PAUL LINDBLAD, PAUL BLAIR.

Seated on Ground — (BATBOYS), GREGG PINDER, JIM PLATTNER, SANDY SALLANDREA.

Official Photo—New York Yankees

"You take a team with twenty-five a--holes, and I'll show you a pennant. I'll show you the New York Yankees."

Bill Lee

The Yankees-Red Sox feud goes back a long way, and few have captured the feelings of Red Sox players and their fans better than former Boston pitcher Bill "Spaceman" Lee. A legendary baseball character, Lee pitched for the Red Sox from 1969 to 1978 and had a front-row seat for Boston's back-to-back second-place finishes to the Bronx Bombers in 1977 and 1978.

Index

"It ain't over till it's over."

Yogi Berra